Paul R. Beeman

THE WORDLESS LANGUAGE LEARNING GUIDE

AN IMAGE BASED APPROACH TO LANGUAGE LEARNING.

LANCER LEARNING COMMUNITIES

Paperback ISBN: 978-1-958941-01-0
Hardcover ISBN: 978-1-958941-03-4
E-Book ISBN: 978-1-958941-02-7

1st Printing July 2022

Lancer Learning Communities, LLC

WWW.LANCERCOMMUNITIES.COM

This book is dedicated to everyone who has been a host in my language journey:

My parents, brothers and sister. Teachers, friends and neighbors. Anne, Daniel, Ahmed, Modou, Mohammad, Hamza, Zouhaira, and Marwa.

A special thanks to my wife, who inspired our journeys overseas and kept me humble as we learned languages together.

This book could not have been created without the groundbreaking research and planning of Dr. Greg Thomson and his wife Angela. Their work developing the Growing Participator Approach has helped tens of thousands of people learn new languages, including myself.

Congratulations, you are about to learn a new language! The Wordless Language Learning Guide was hand crafted to give you and your language host 22 days of language learning experiences. When you have finished working through this book, you will be able to understand basic phrases at the market, introduce yourself and describe simple scenes in your new language. But don't stop there! This book is just the beginning of your language journey.

ABOUT THIS BOOK

I love learning languages! From 2013 to 2022, I learned French, Wolof and Tunisian Arabic. I studied in the classroom, in my living room and on the streets. However, each time I started a new language, I felt like I was missing a tool.

We learn our mother tongue from observation. There is no translation, our minds naturally sort through the sounds we hear and eventually assign meaning. This process shapes our minds, turning us into native speakers.

It is possible to have native fluency in multiple languages. The trick is to eliminate translation so that the mind can do it's work of figuring out the new language. Before the alphabet, before hieroglyphics, humans used images to record concepts. These simple images are called logographs. By using logographs in language learning, we enable the mind to link concepts directly with sounds, avoiding the need for translation.

This guide is a curriculum that uses logographs to lead you and your language host into your new language. Each logograph in this book has been hand designed to elicit the most elementary of concepts in any language. Your language host will decide the words that best fit each image and impart them to you. These images have been organized onto pages and into units to maximize your learning. As you work through these logographs, get creative. Use real items and actions so that the new words take shape in your mind.

Learning a language requires hundreds of hours of interaction, studying and schooling. You are about to become a growing participator in a new language. As you explore this book, keep in mind that each language and culture is unique. Your new language will have new sounds, grammar and maybe even tones. As you go through this book with your host, keep your ears open and attuned to these new sounds. They are the building blocks your mind needs to learn this new language.

Bon Courage,

Paul R. Beeman

INSTRUCTIONS

HOW TO BE A GREAT HOST

The core belief behind this book is that with the right tools anyone can teach their language. The host is someone who welcomes the learner into their world by sharing their language. Here are some qualities that make a great language host:

- They are native speakers or have native fluency.

- They are patient. Just as a parent must be patient with their child, a language host needs to be patient with the participant. It will take much repetition and work before they see results.

- They understand what it is like to learn another language. When a person has learned another language, they have a better understanding of what makes their language unique.

- They are someone the participant trusts. Language hosts and participants often create a tight bond from the time they spend together. By the time the host and participant have finished this book, they will feel like family.

- They speak slowly and naturally.

- They speak to the participant using words the participant understands.

HOW TO BE A GREAT LEARNER

Anyone can learn language. It's true that linguistic training and natural ability can help someone learn a new language but the best language learners do not depend on these. When it is all said and done, the greatest language learners are motivated, humble and determined.

To be a great language learner, figure out what motivates you. Why do you want to learn the language in the first place? Take note and allow that to push you through the tough days.

Be humble. You are starting life over in a new language. You will be laughed at, corrected and maybe even yelled at. This is normal. You are brand new in the language and you are bound to make mistakes. Accept yourself as a beginner and use your mistakes to your advantage.

Be determined. You will not be able to succeed in a new culture unless you learn it's language. Giving up is never an option if you want to be a functioning participant in a new culture.

HOW TO USE THIS BOOK

Wordless is an image guided language learning curriculum that is designed to introduce learners to basic concepts in a new language. It is divided into 22 units. Each unit consists of the maximum quantity of new material that a language learner should try to learn in one day. These units are identified with hand signals, with the number of fingers extended indicating the unit number. While some learners may take multiple days to finish a unit, only one unit should be introduced per day.

The first 10 lessons are a crucial time for the learner. They should not try to speak the new language during these first 10 meetings. All languages have unique sounds, rhythms and structures. Taking time to listen is essential for the learner in order to hear these novelties.

Each page contains a manageable quantity of new concepts. When they are being studied, hosts should follow a pattern of **introduction**, **repetition**, **verification** and **recording**.

Introduction is when the host presents a logograph for the first time. There are logographs for common *phrases, objects, verbs* and *descriptive* words.

Phrases. A phrase is depicted using a scene with speech bubbles. Scenes portray daily interactions the learner will encounter in their new language community. Examples of phrases in the first unit are "Hello", "How are you?", and "Goodbye". If there are multiple phrases for the same idea, the language host should only introduce the most common one.

Objects. These should be introduced with an indicative phrase and article. For example, in English, when introducing the logograph of the man, the host should point to the logograph of the man and say "Man. This is a man." By putting the noun in an indicative phrase, the host also introduces the learner to the way their language indicates.

Verbs. Circular frames indicate a verb or action concept. These should be introduced in the base form. For example, in English, "Stand, Walk, Run". After the learner has a grasp of these base forms, then it would be appropriate to start using the verbs in present form during review. For example, phrases like "The man walks" or "I walk" may be used in the verification stage.

Descriptive. These may appear in an image with prompts ("such as under", "next to" and "in front") or in a square with a rounded bottom. They are to be introduced in their neutral form (if it exists).

After introducing each concept, the language host will **repeat** their introductions of the concepts until the learner is confident enough to start interacting with the content.

The **verification** part of the lesson is a great opportunity to be creative and have fun. In initial sessions, at least 40 minutes of every hour should be spent in activities that verify a learner's understanding. Here are some examples of activities to help the learner grow in their understanding:

> *Dirty Dozen*: There are approximately a dozen words on each page. After introduction the language host asks the participant where words are on the page. For example, "Where is the man?" "Where is the woman?", or "Where is 'hello'?". The learner will point to the corresponding picture.

Simon Says: The host says an action or phrase and the participant performs it.

Search and Find: Use real objects or the composite images in this book to play search and find. The language host may ask the participant to find objects or perform actions. These composite images can also be used as references for you to start describing scenes.

Memory: The language host says a phrase and the participant points to the object(s) and actions in the book that correspond to the phrase. For example, in unit one, "The man walks". The learner will point to the man and walks. It should also be mentioned that performing this activity helps a learner to start forming the new language's grammar in their mind.

Recording is the final, most important part of each page. Having a recording of the spoken words with images, gives the learner the freedom to review what they have learned between sessions. If video recording is not available, an audio recording will suffice as long as the learner has a copy of the book and the words are presented in order of those on the page.

In order to maximize learning, language sessions should never deviate from the language being studied. Vocabulary of affirmation and correction such as "yes, no, good, great job and wonderful" should be used as often as possible. As the host and learner interact, these types of phrases should flow naturally from the host and the participant will benefit from the constant encouragement. No translation is necessary for these words, the learner will naturally figure out what the host is trying to communicate.

Review of previous concepts should be done before moving on to a new page. This means that the first part of each lesson should involve review of the previous words covered. After a page is completed, it should be reviewed with concepts learned in the previous pages. The learner needs this constant repetition and the host should be prepared to repeat the same words over and over again hundreds of times.

Review is also a great time to highlight words that are close in sound. For example, in English we have "Pen" and "Pan". These are not on the same page. When review is performed, the learner becomes aware of the difference between close sounding words and starts to differentiate between new sounds in the language.

Finally, get out of the book. This book is a guide. For the best language learning experience, incorporate physical objects and role playing into language learning sessions. The book is after all, just one of your tools as you learn the new language.

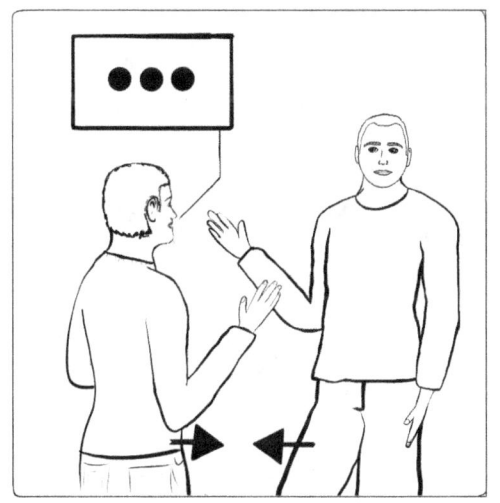
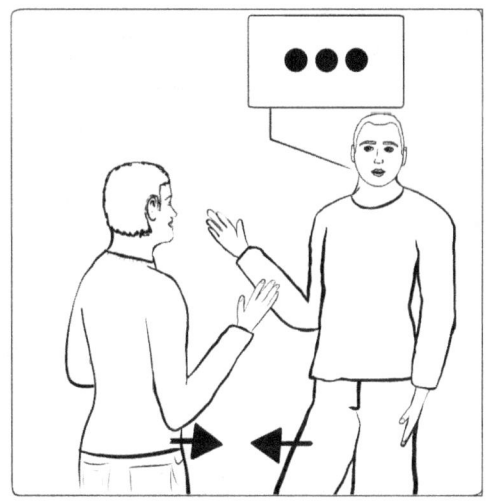

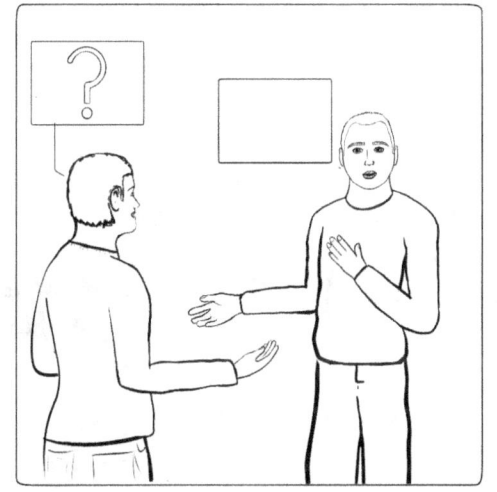

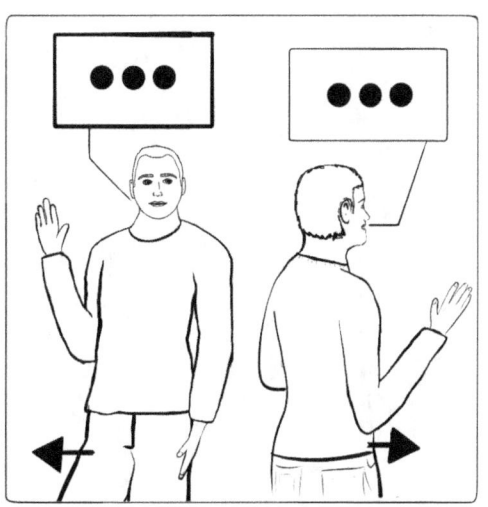

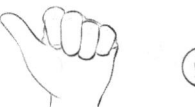

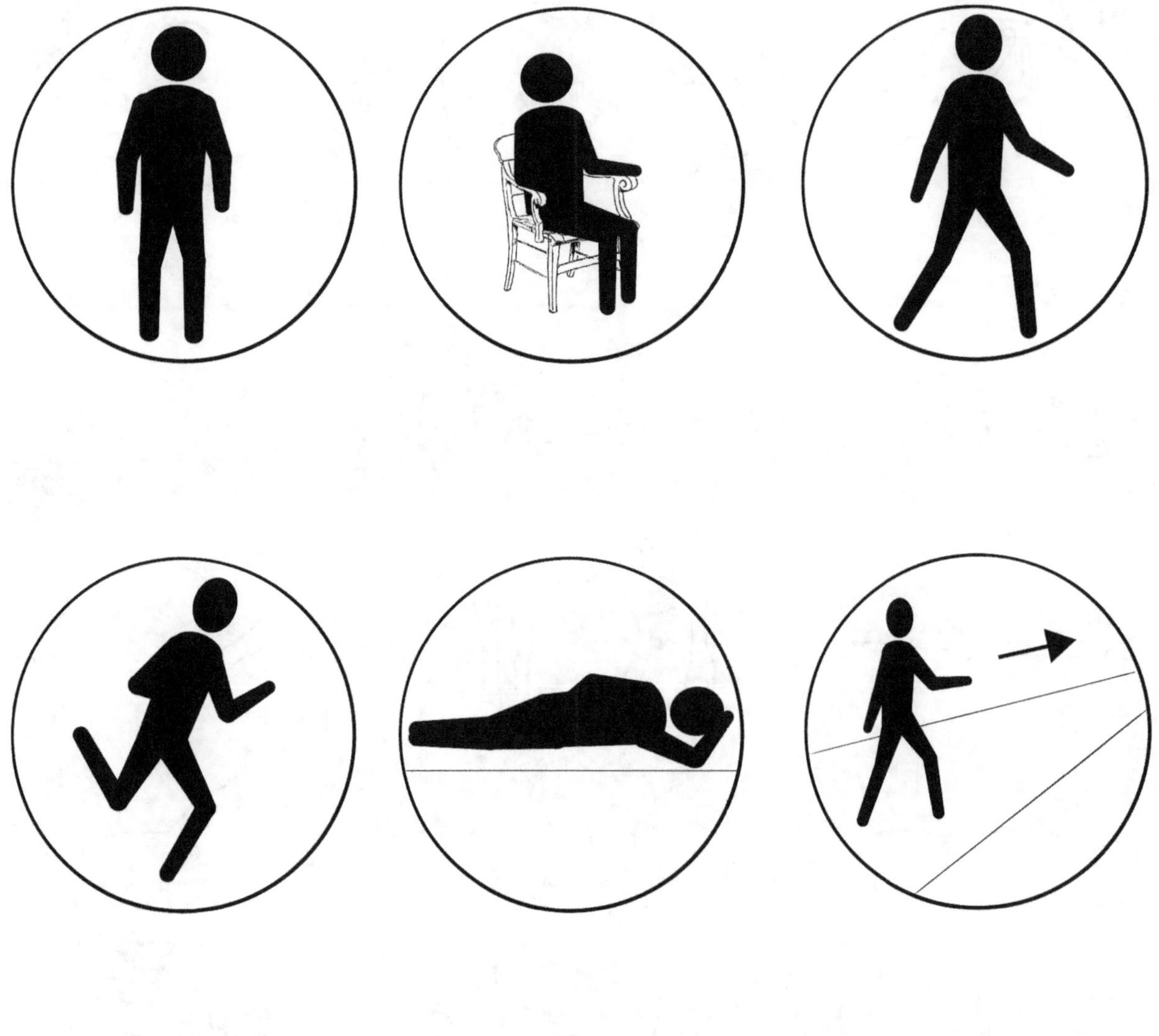

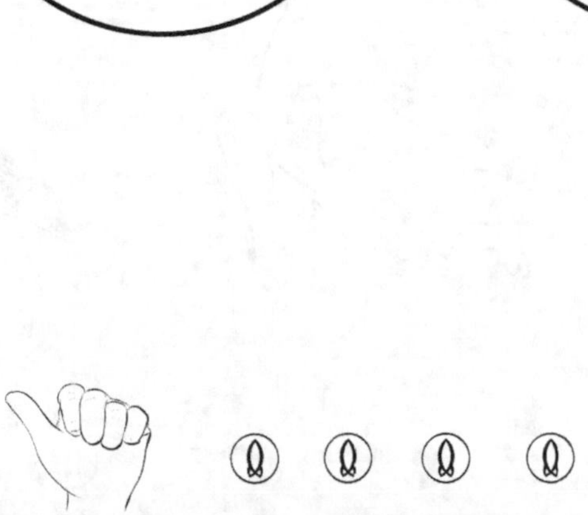

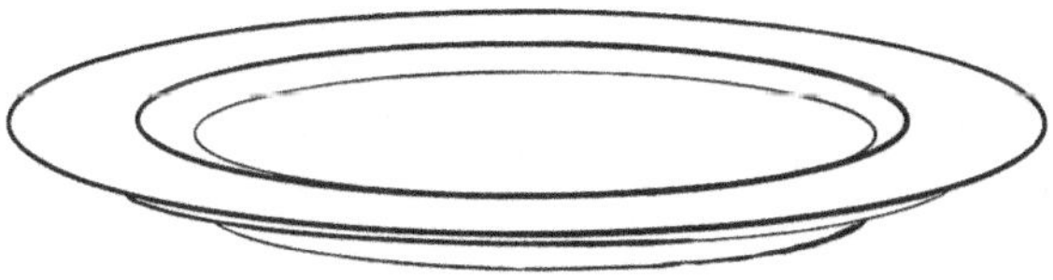

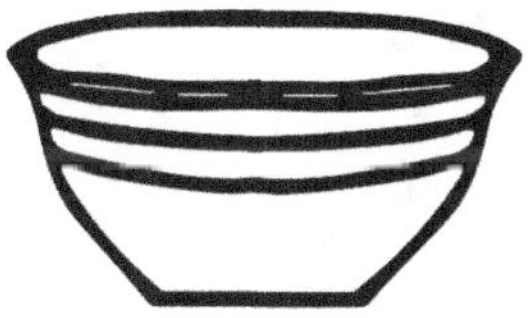

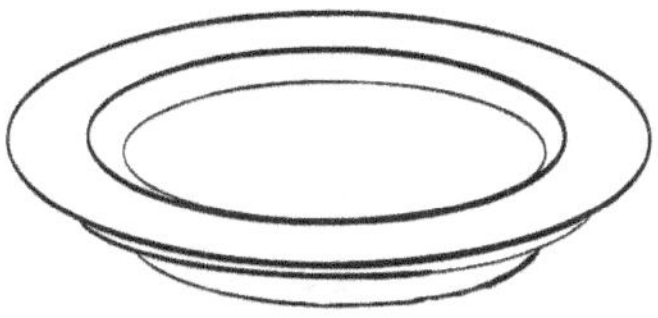

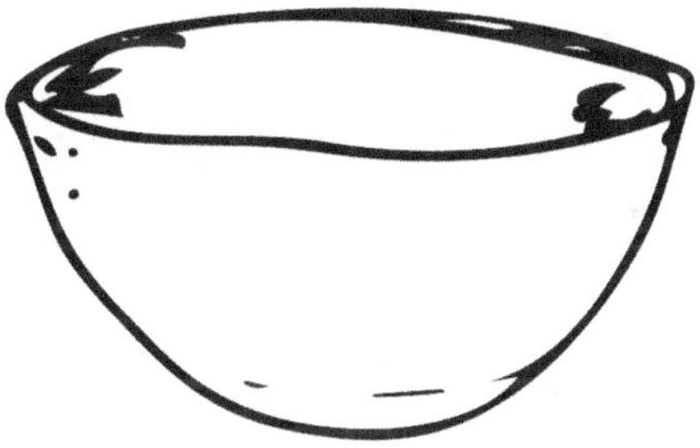

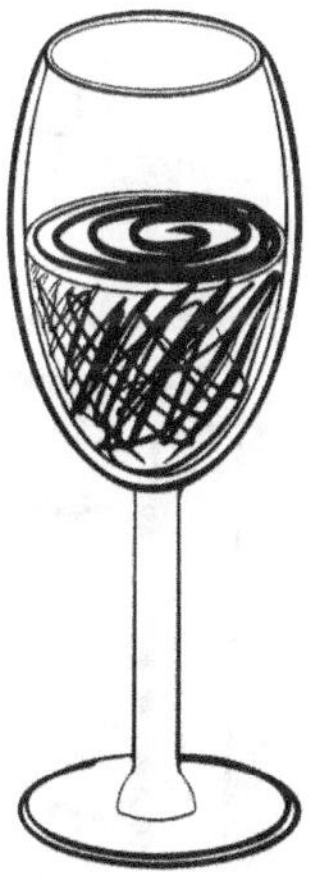

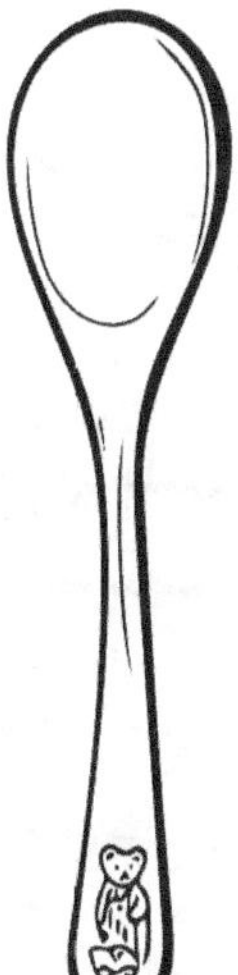

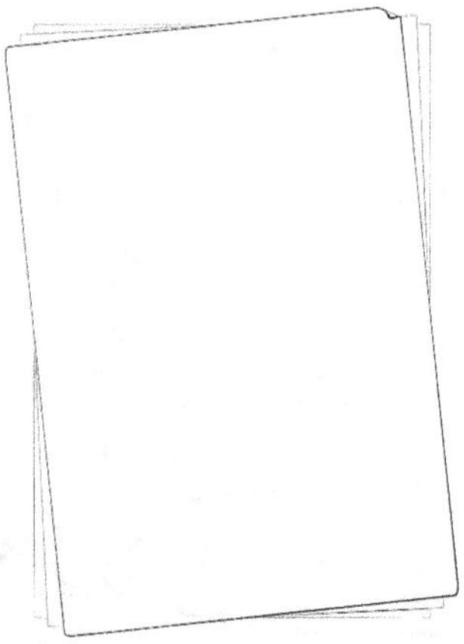

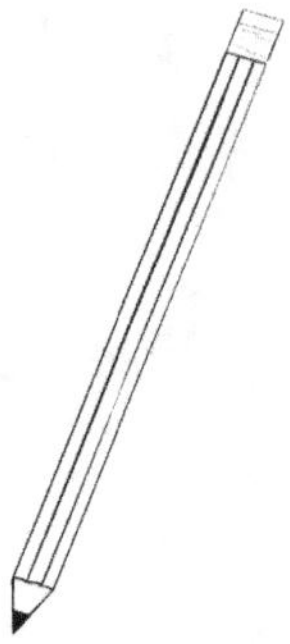

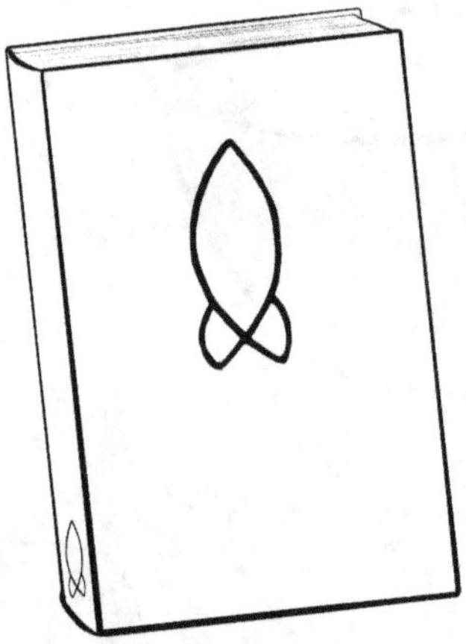

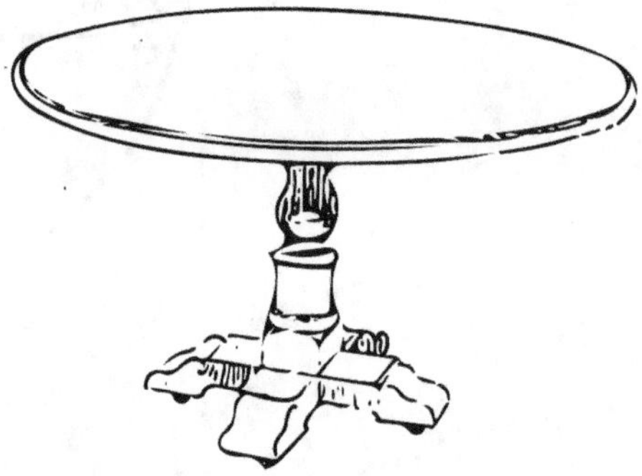

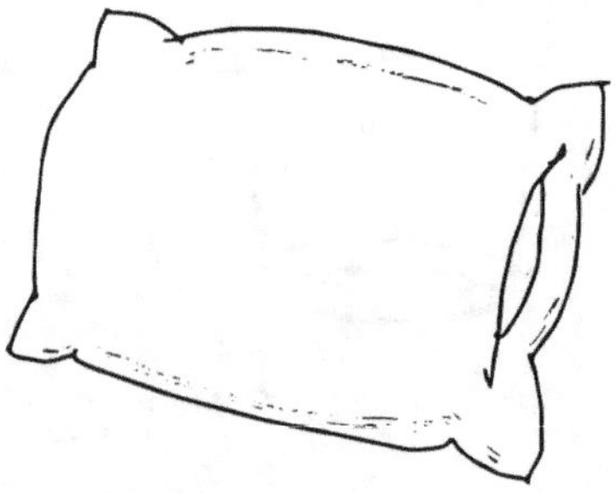

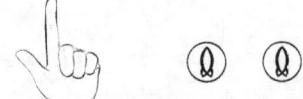

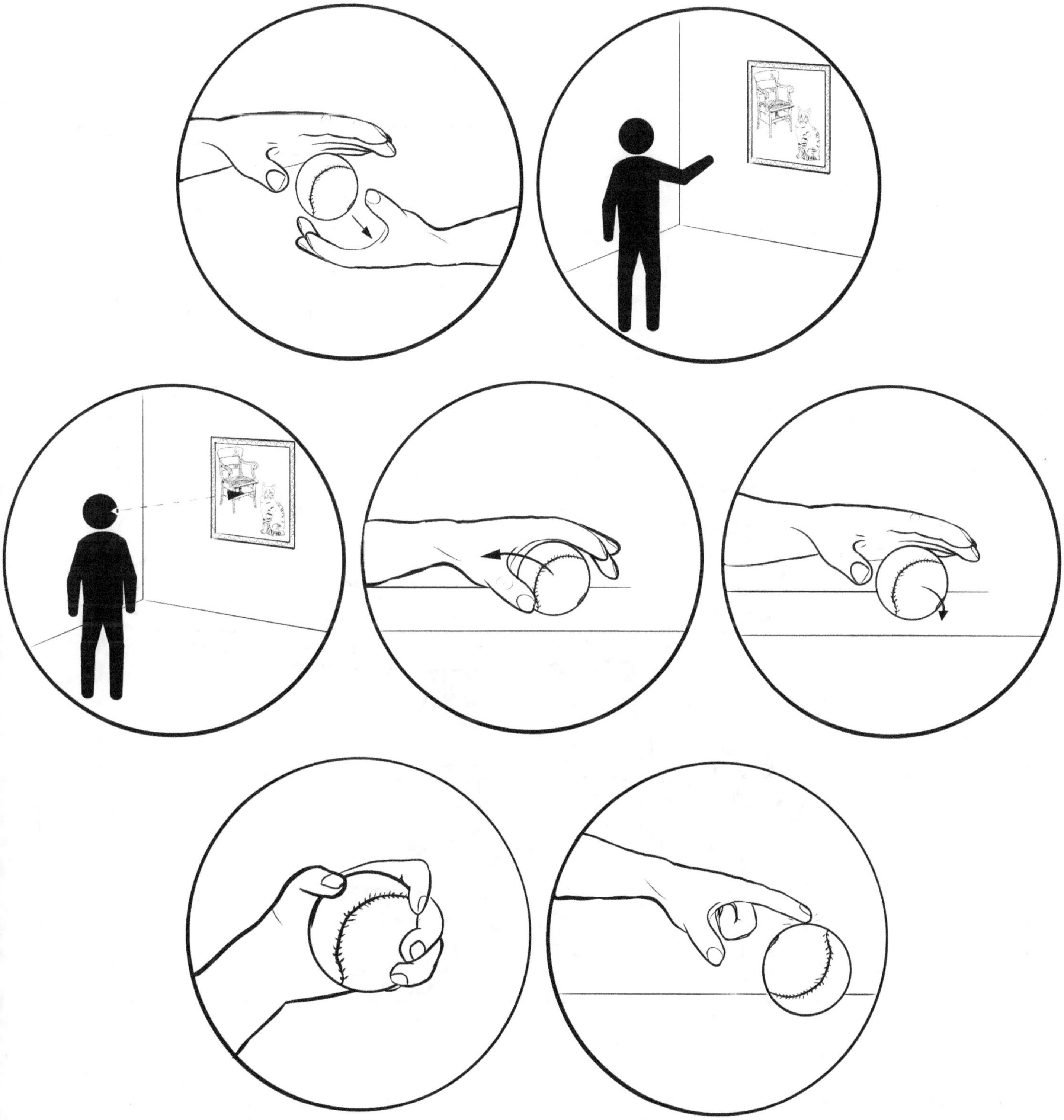

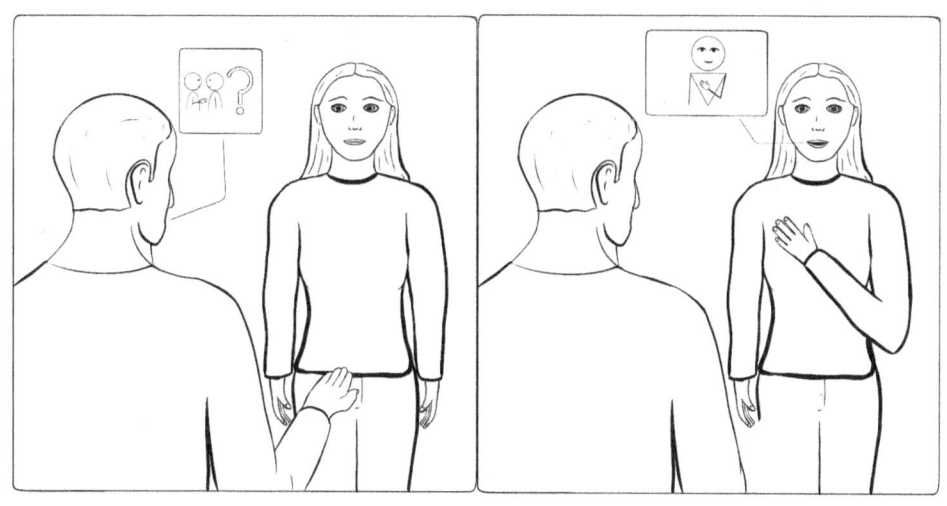

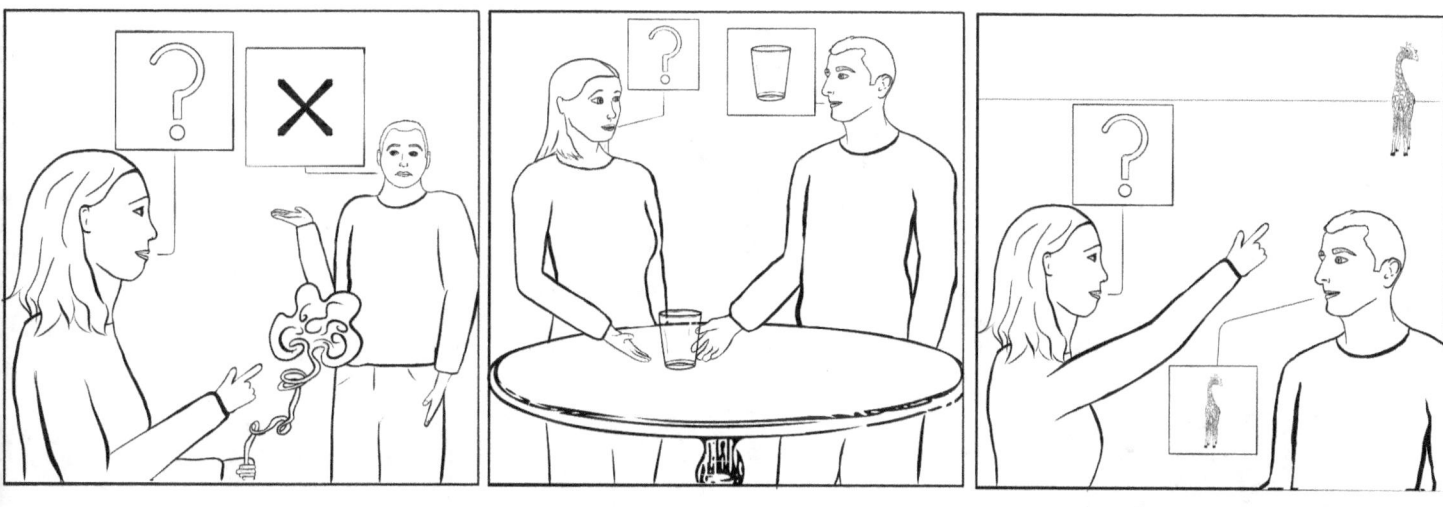

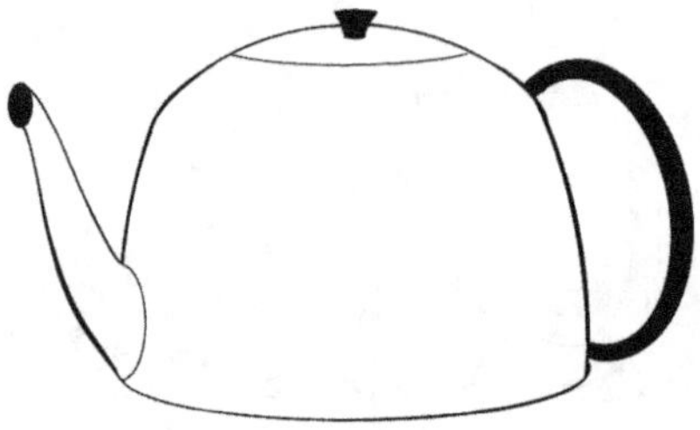

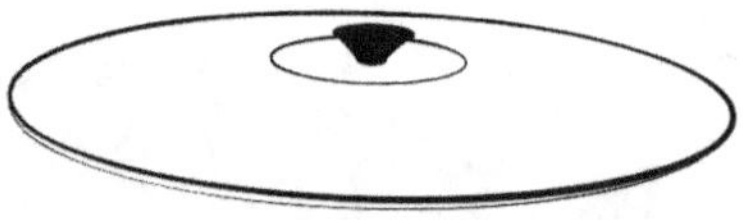

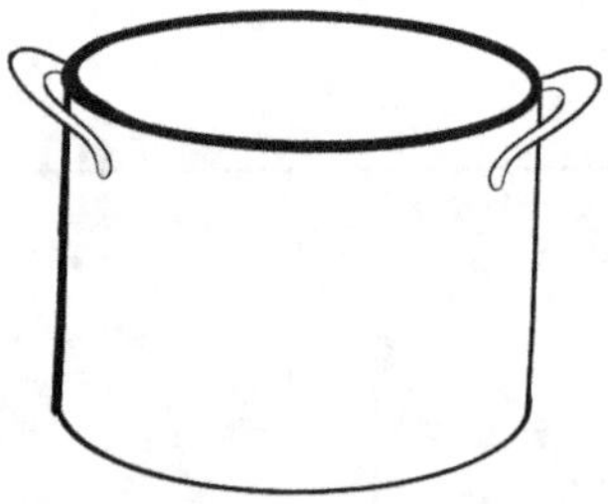

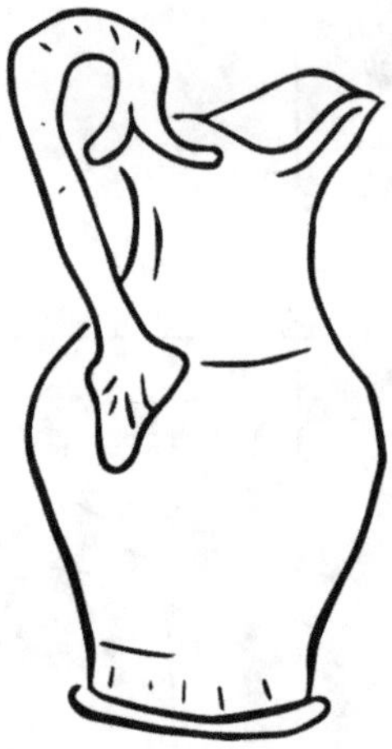

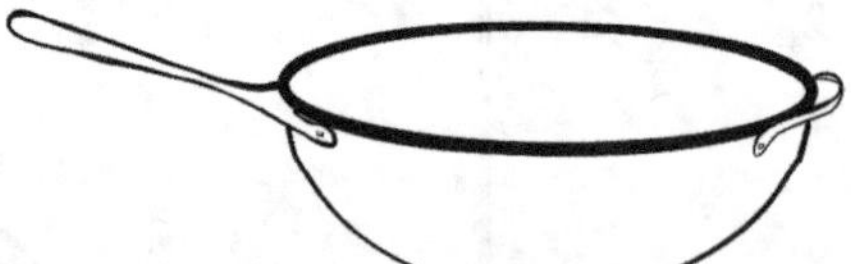

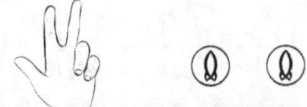

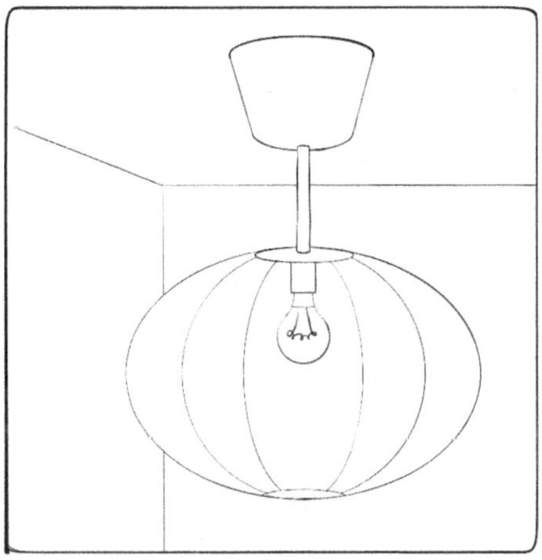

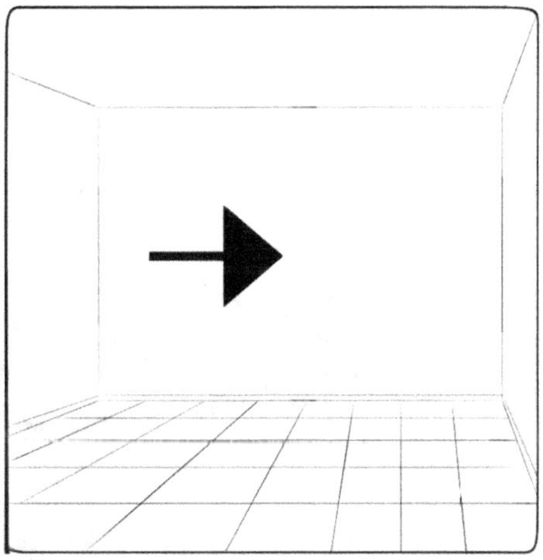

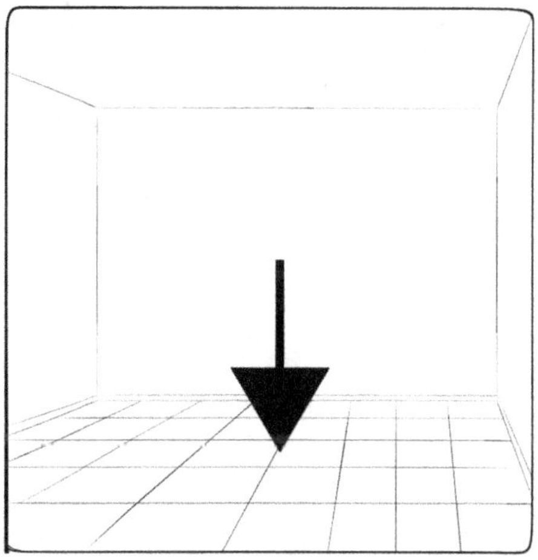

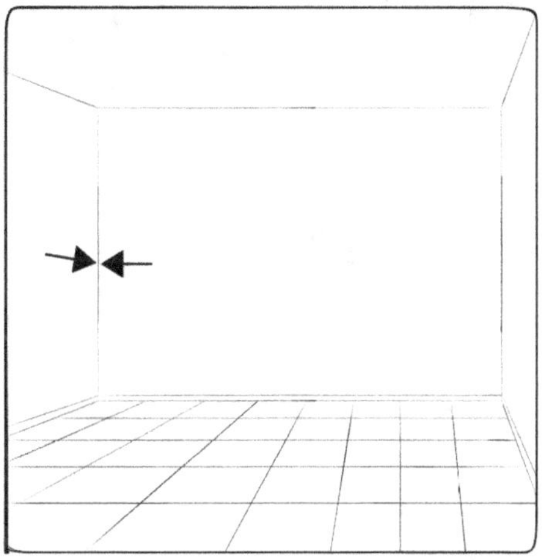

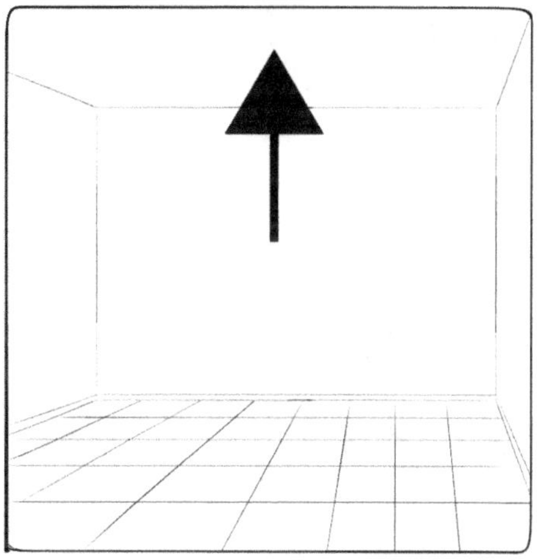

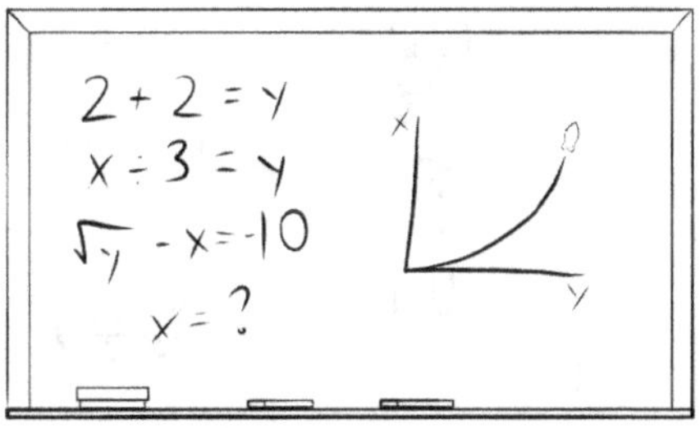

2 + 2 = y
x ÷ 3 = y
√y - x = -10
x = ?

13

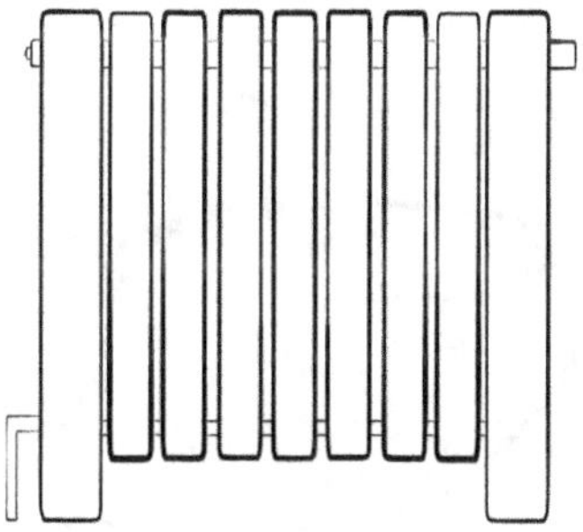

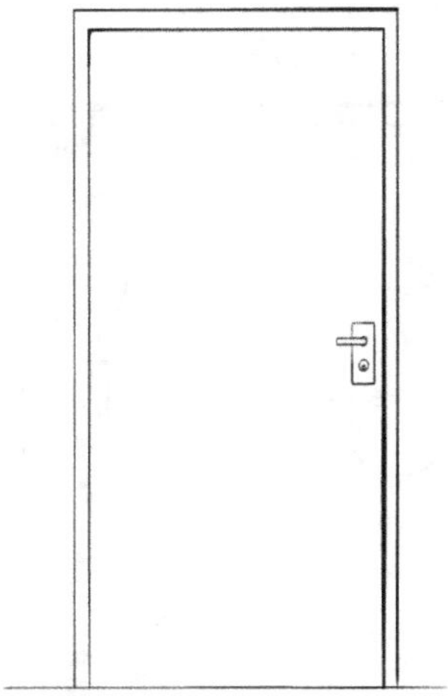

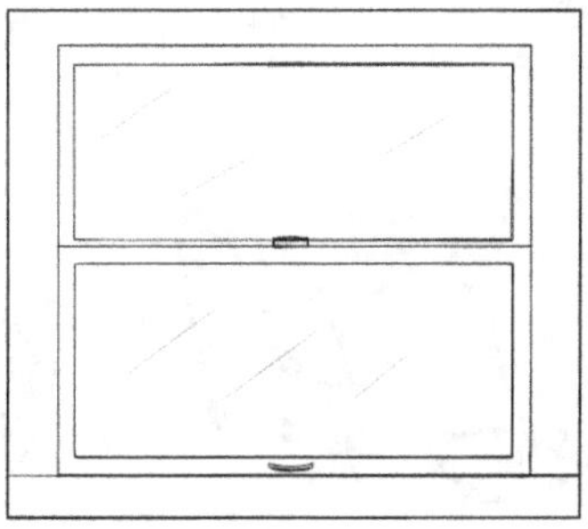

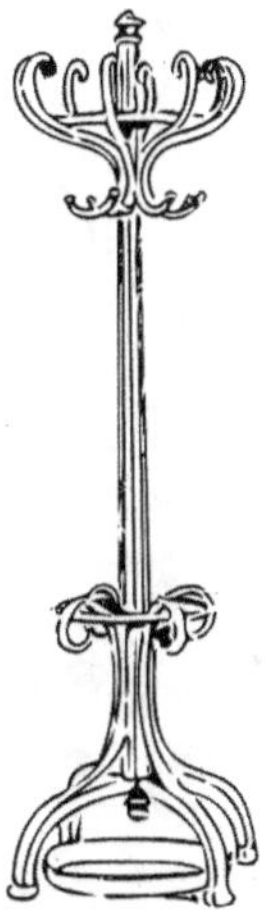

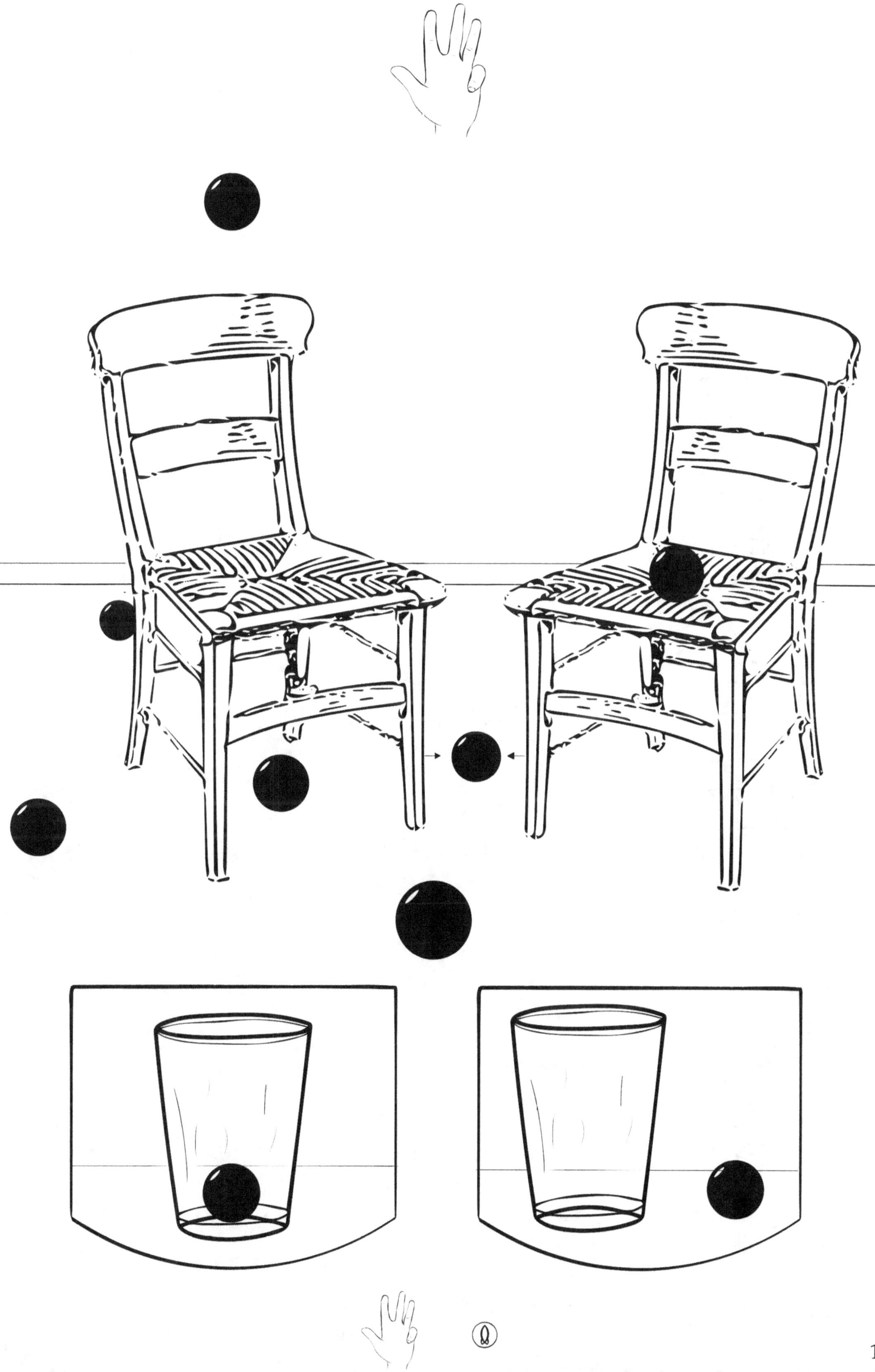

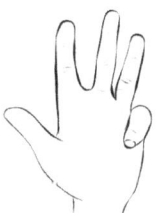

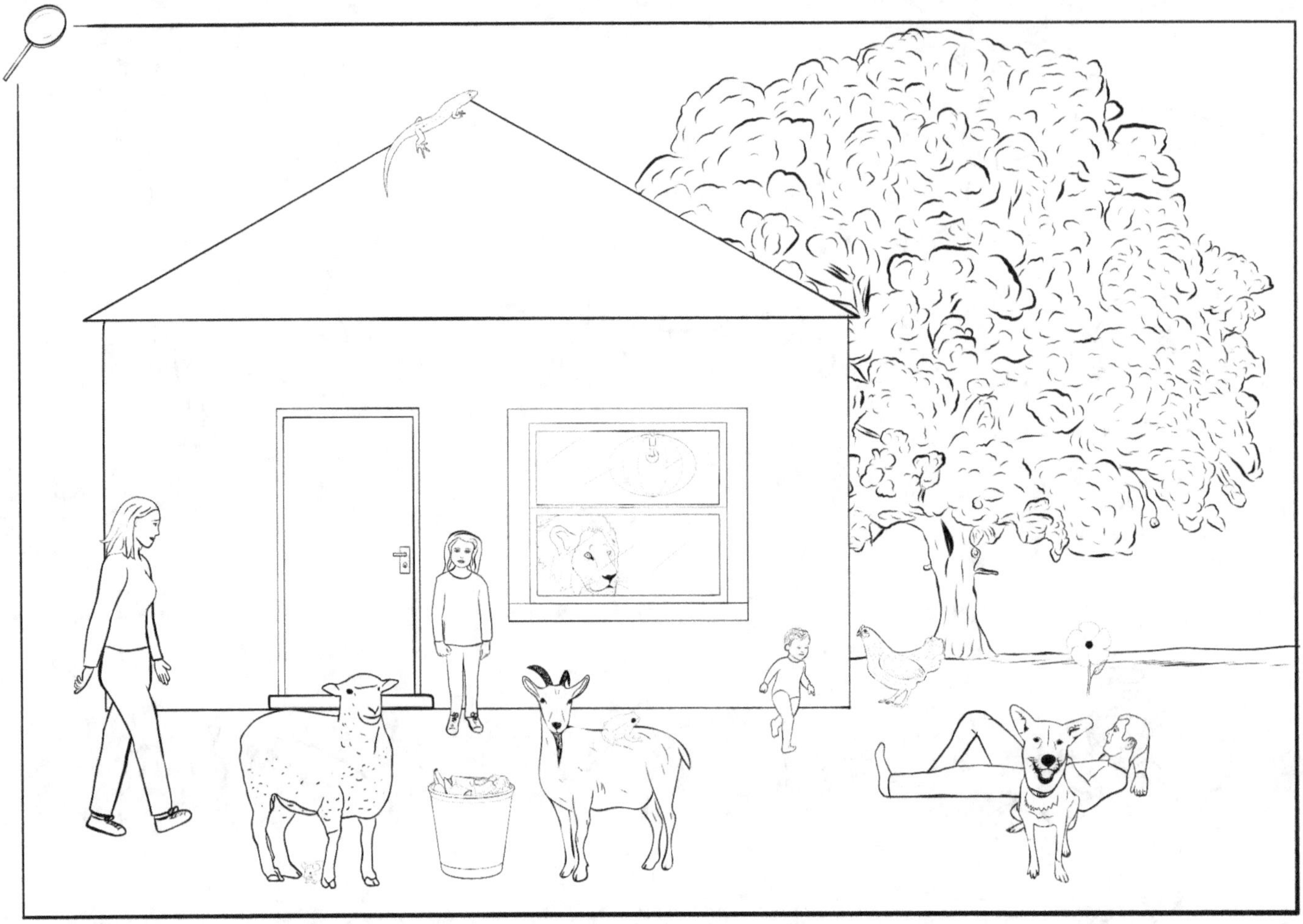

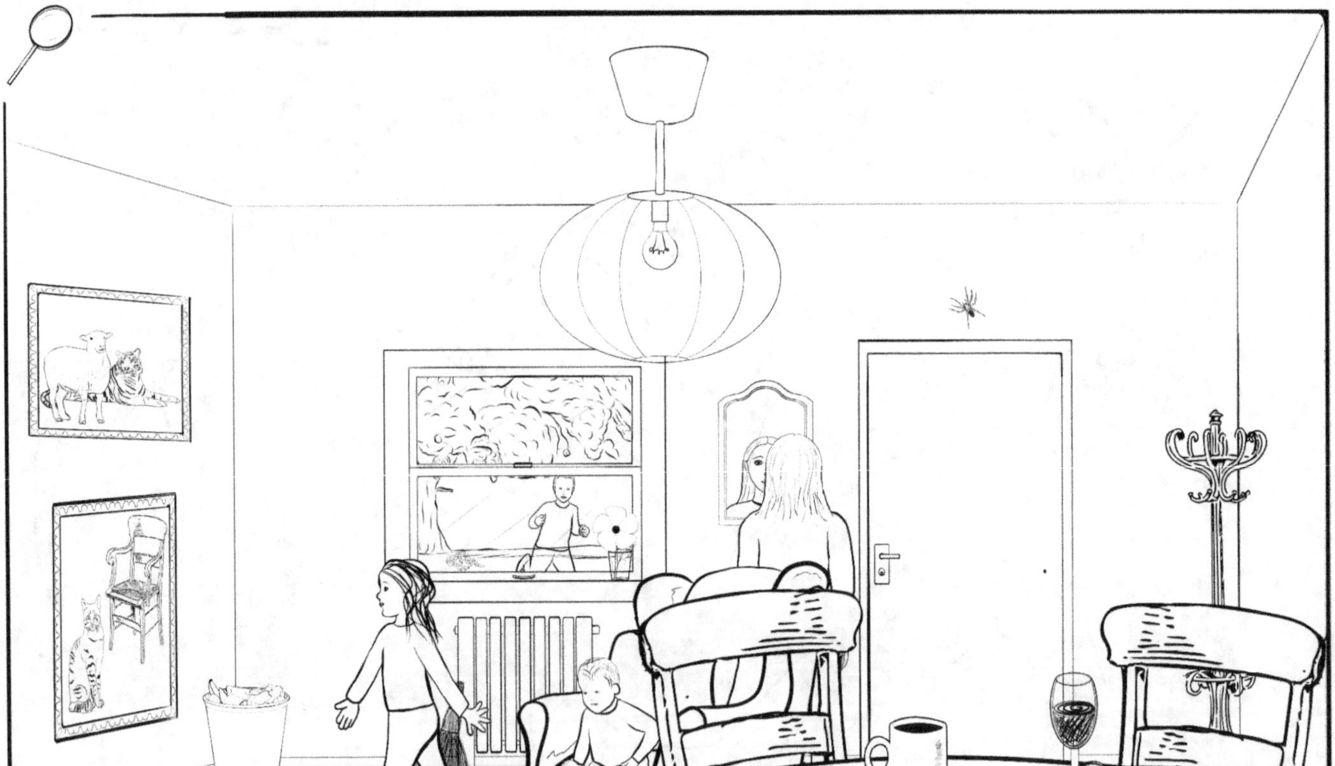

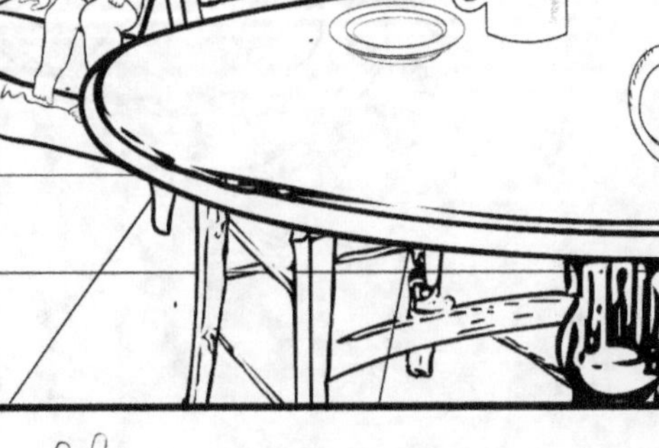

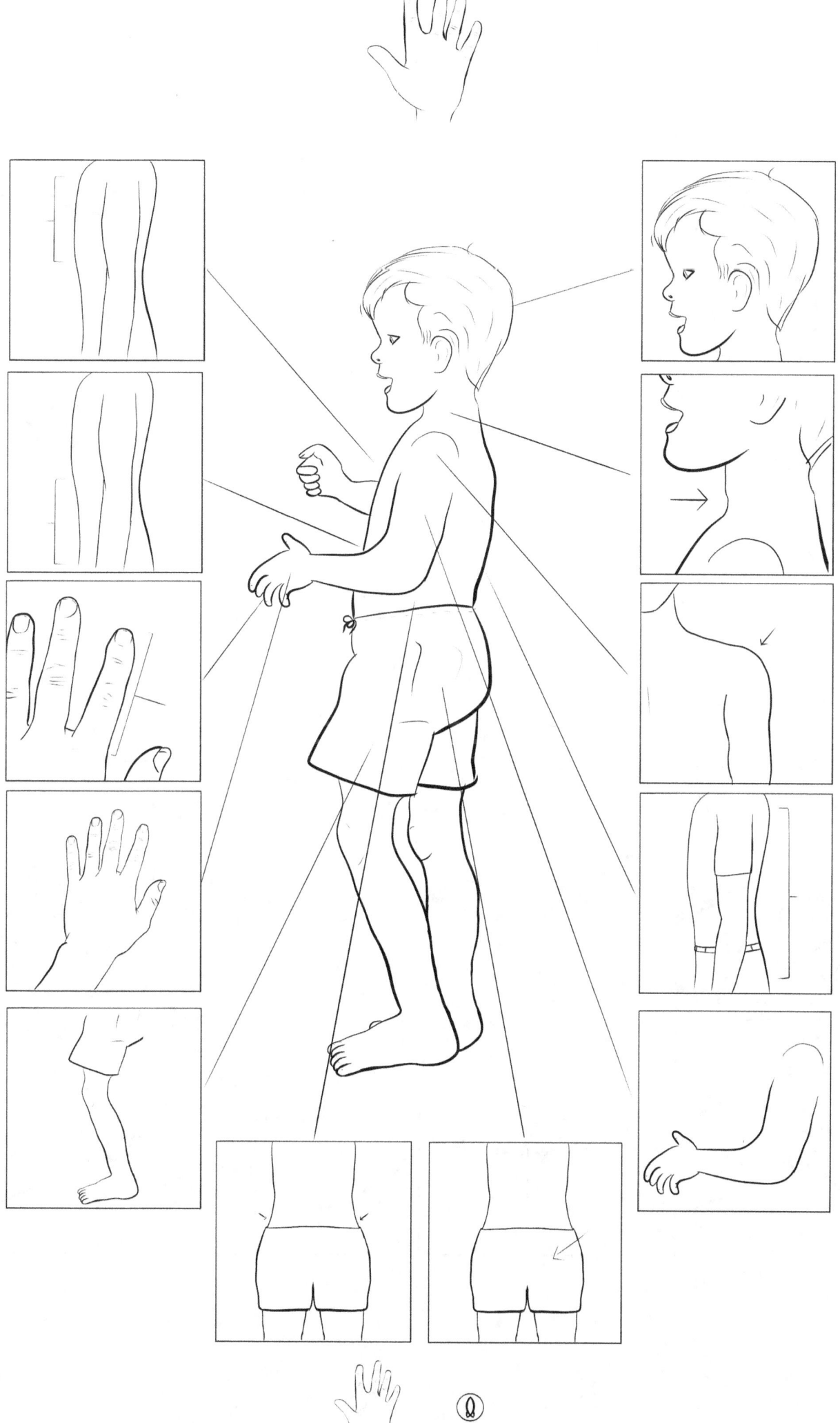

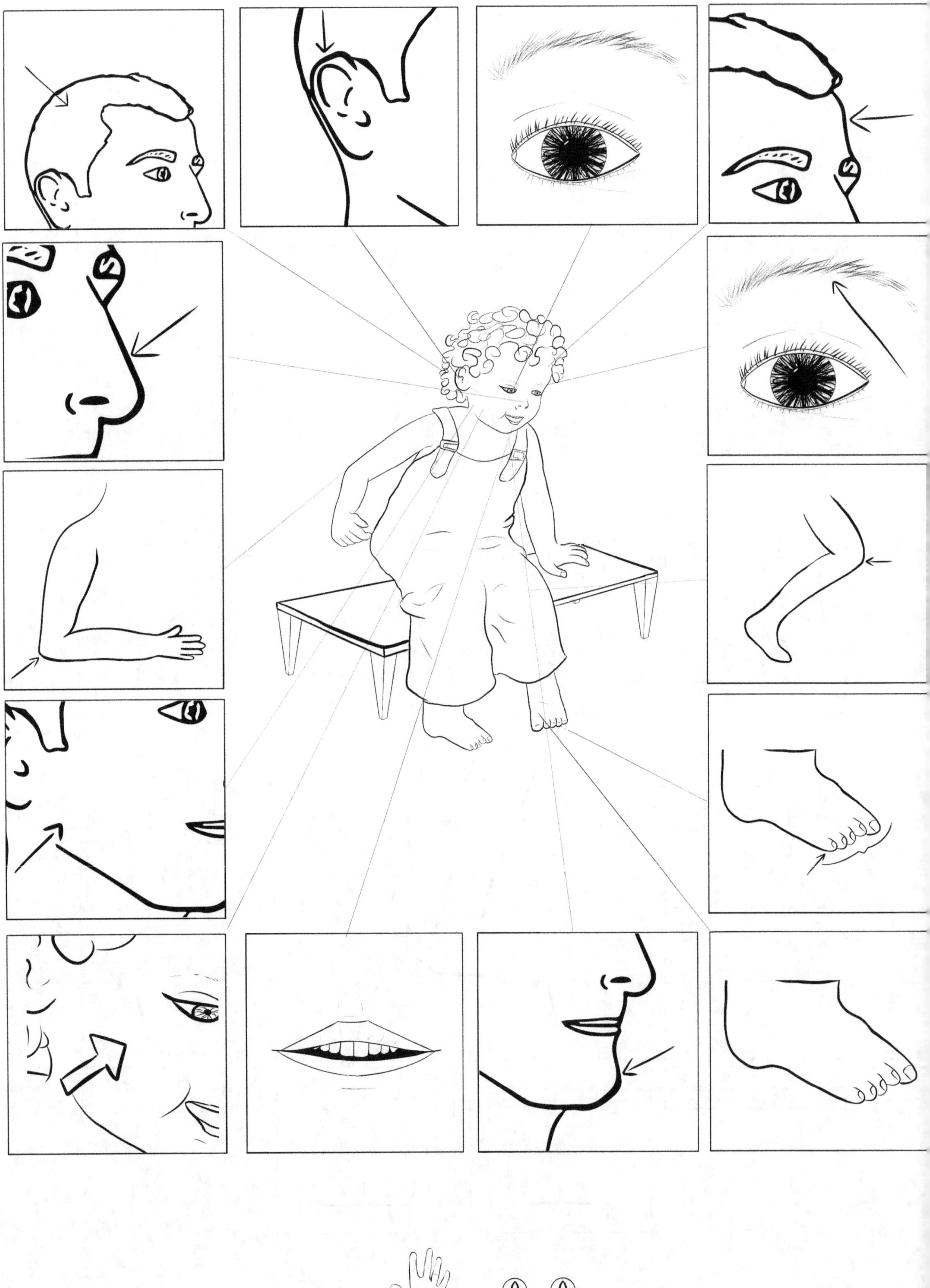

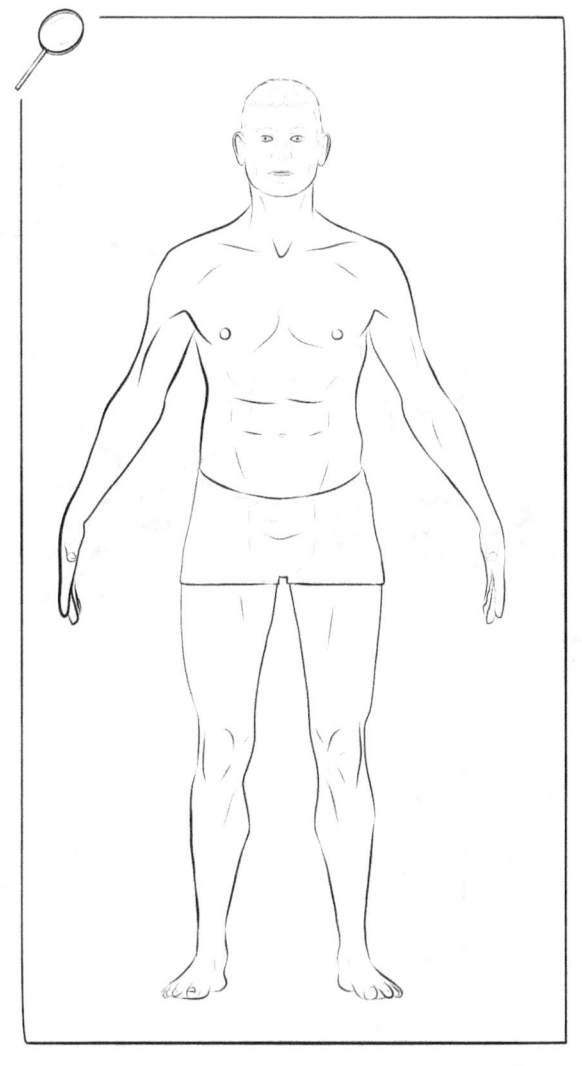

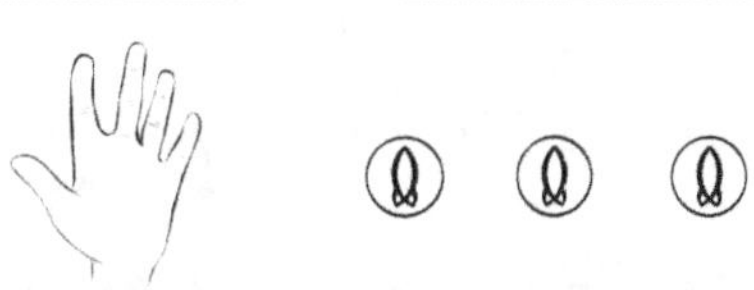

22

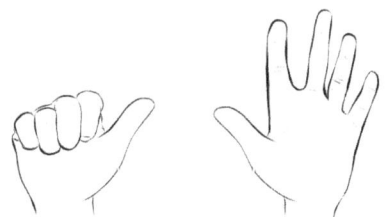

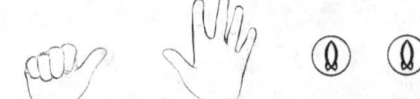

27

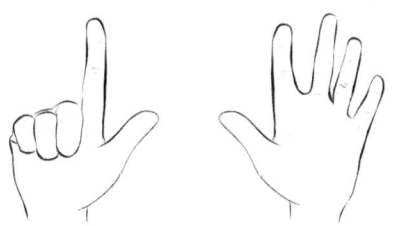

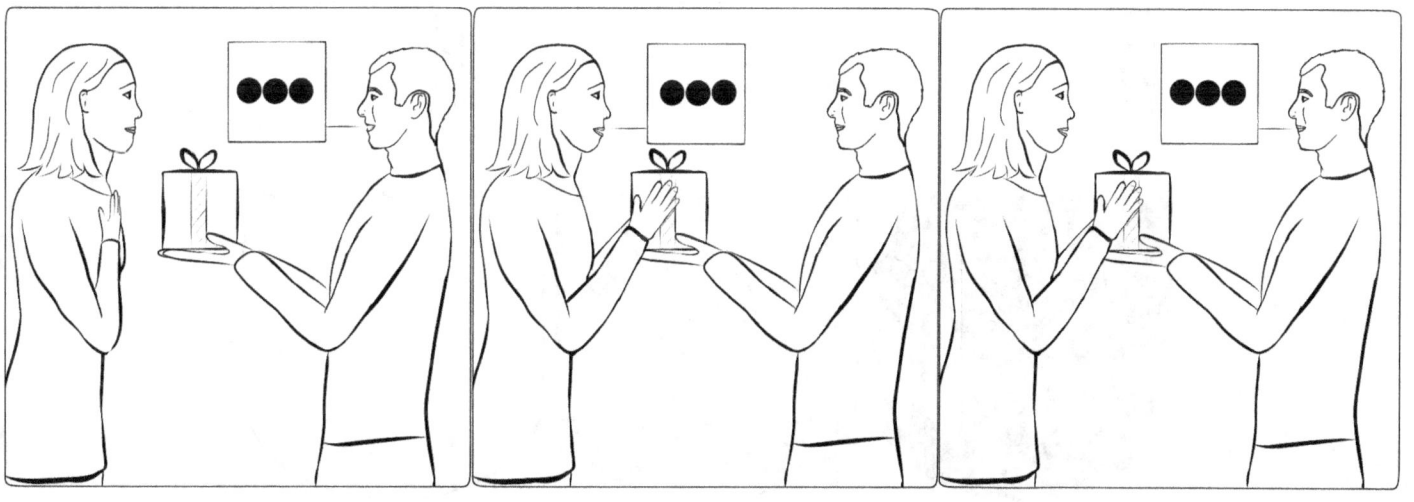

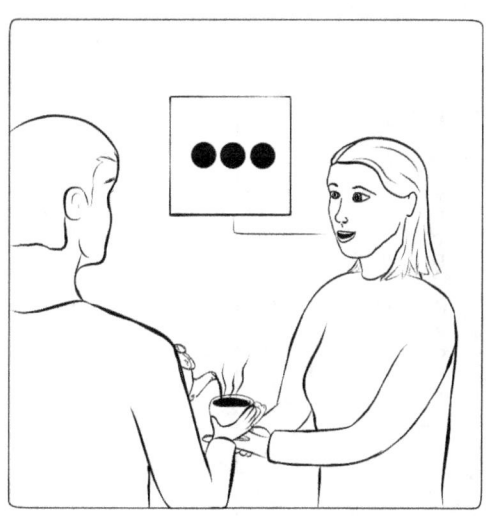

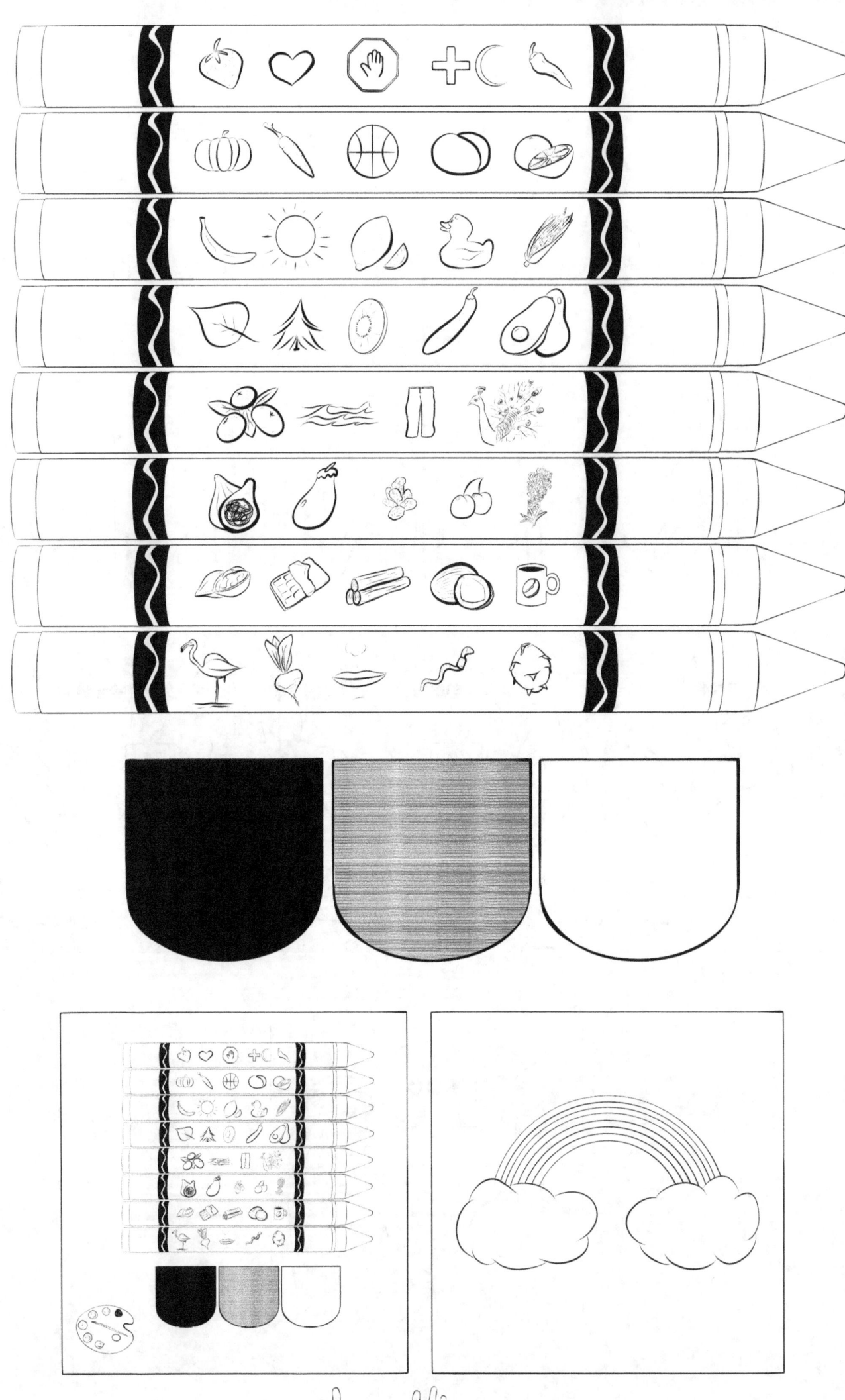

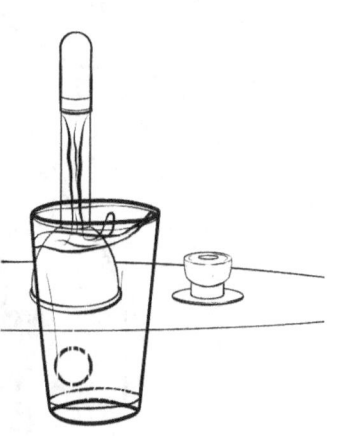

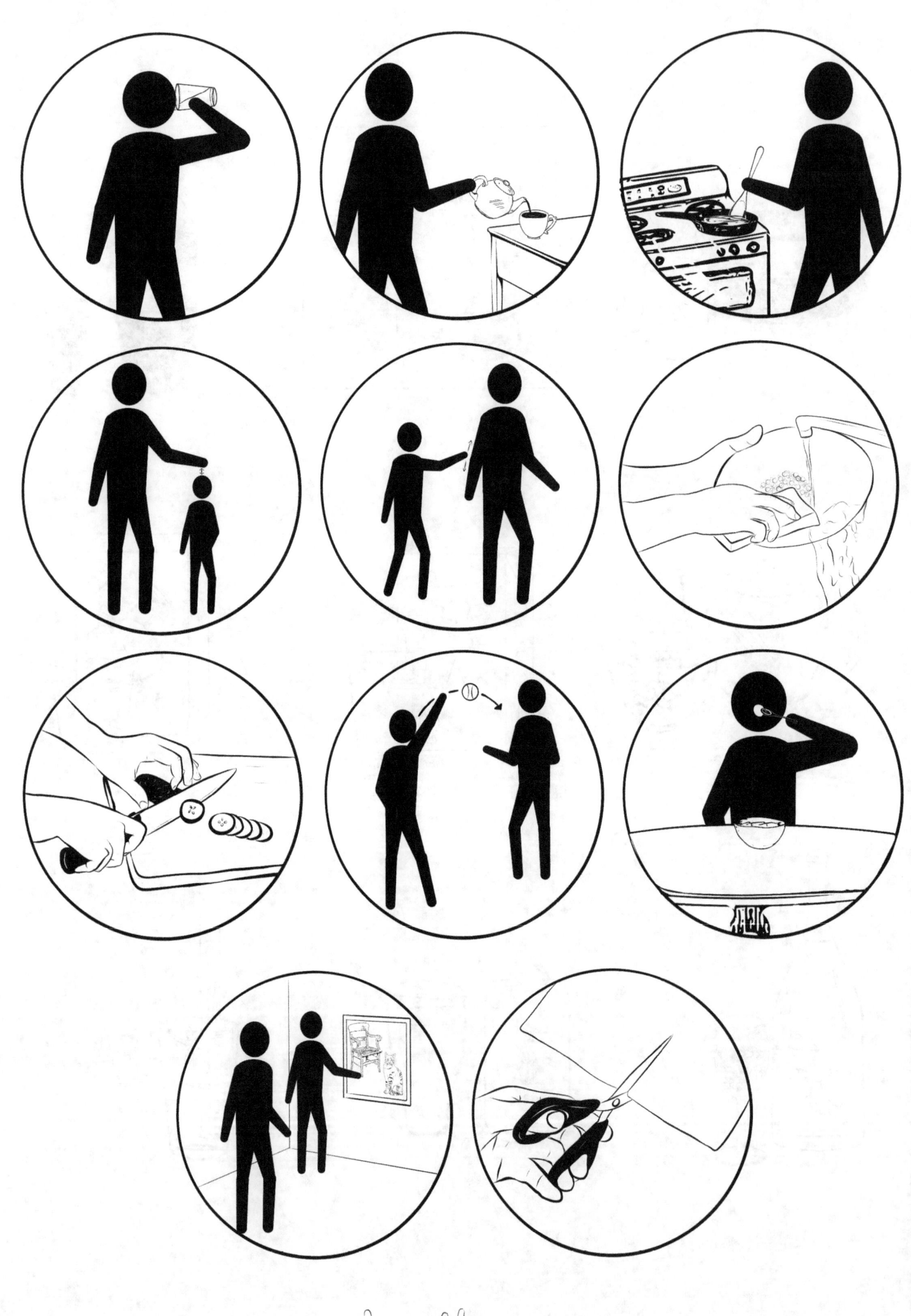

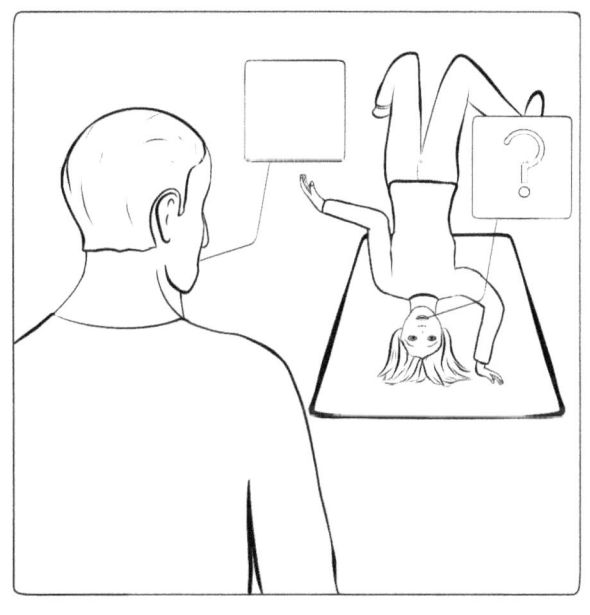

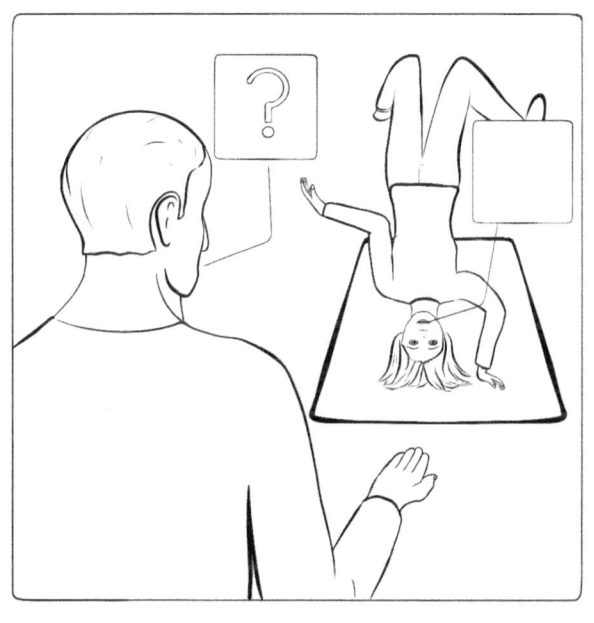
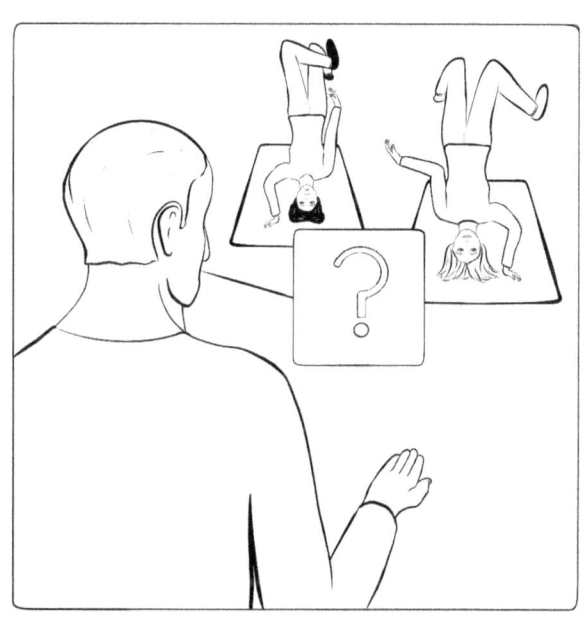

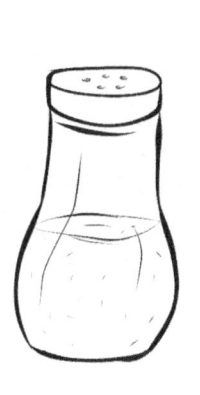

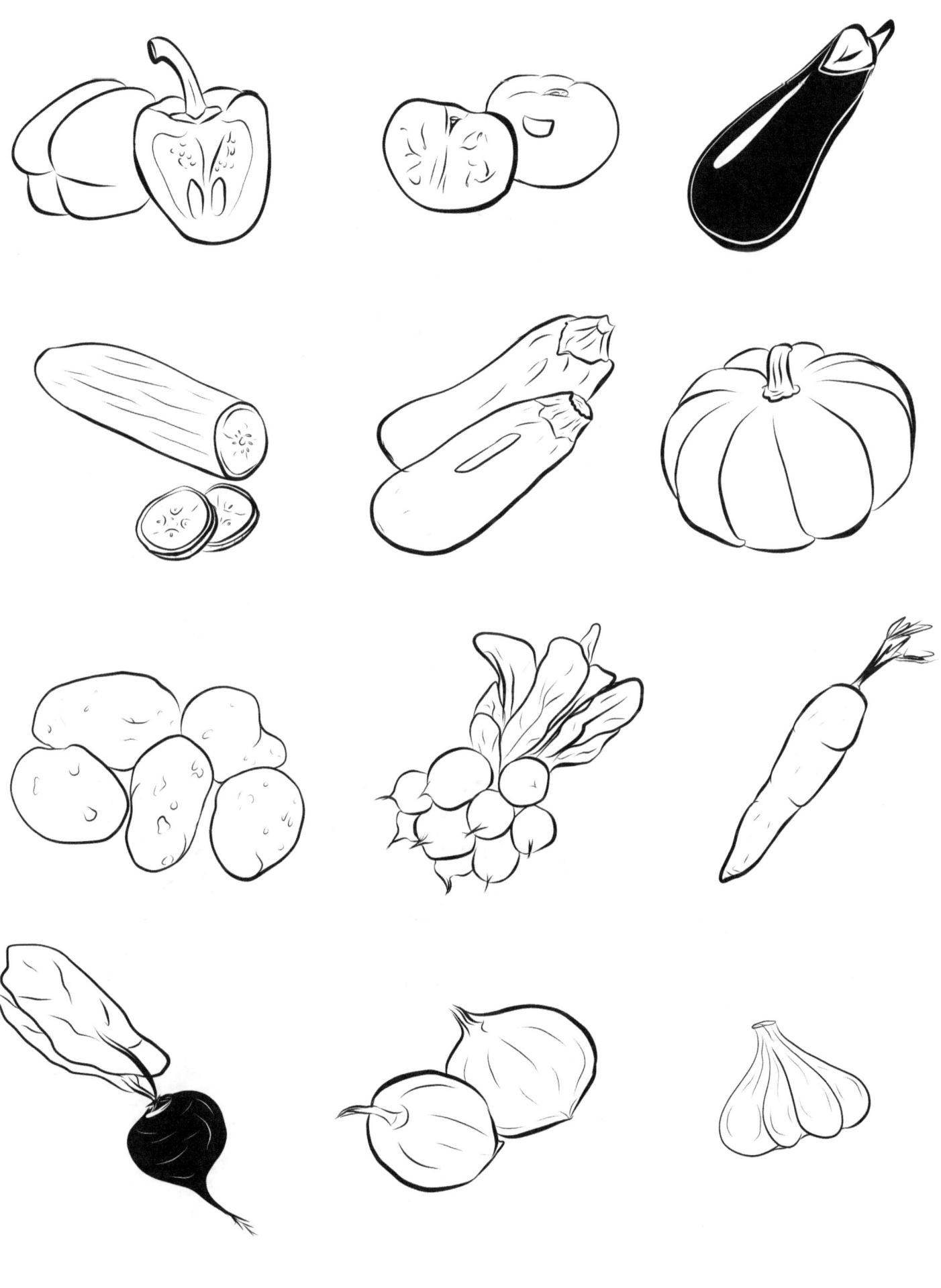

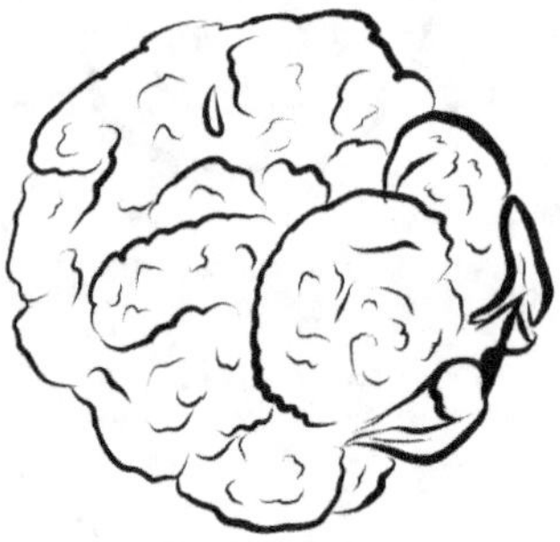

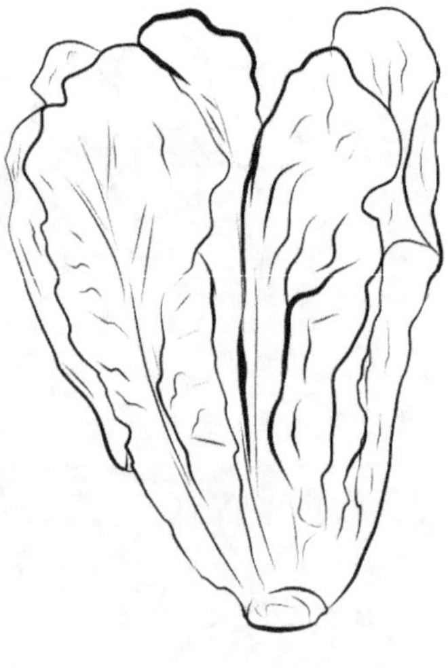

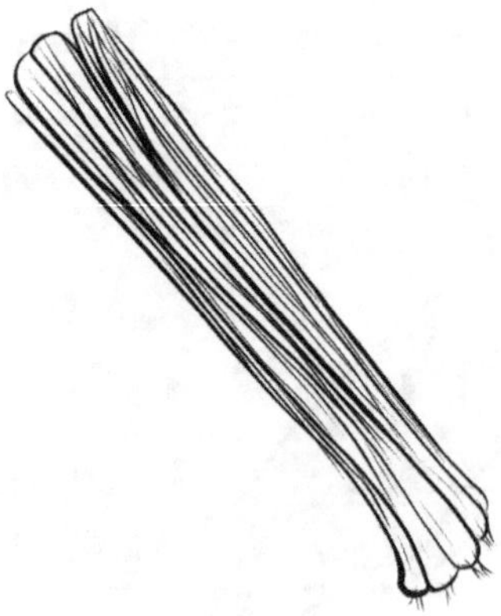

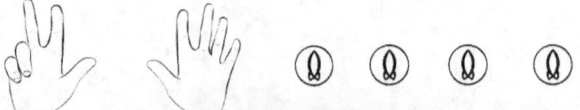

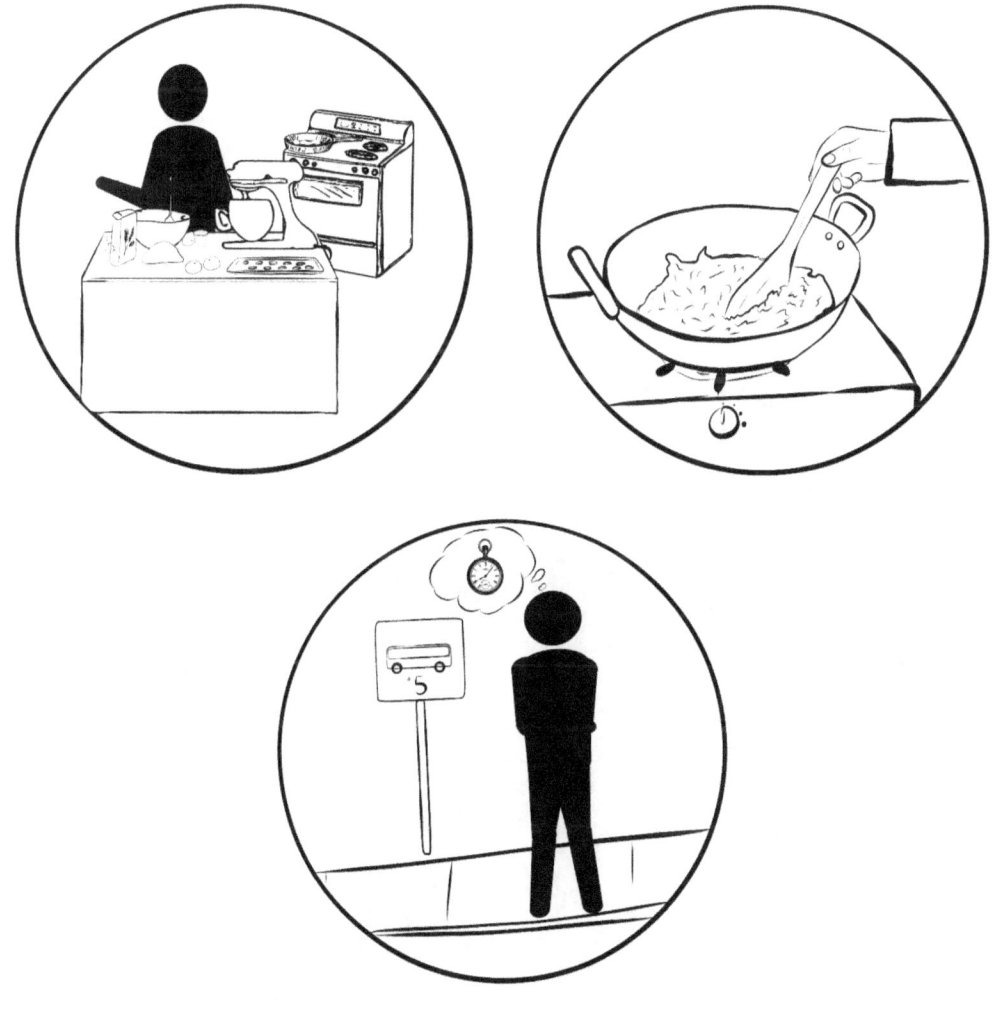

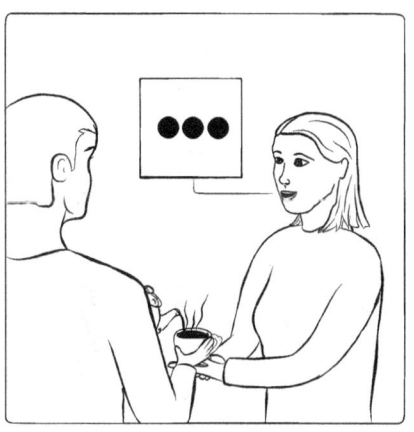
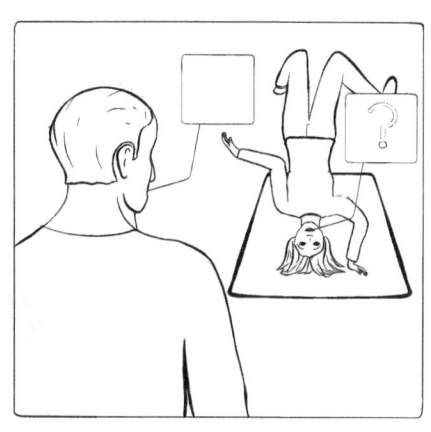

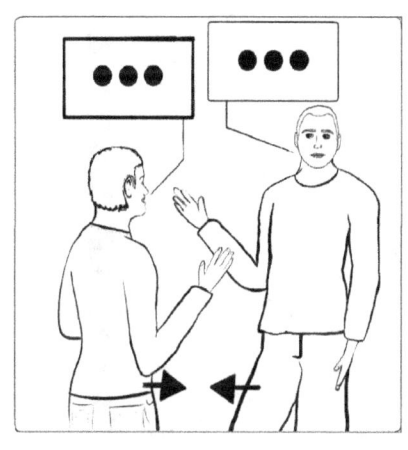

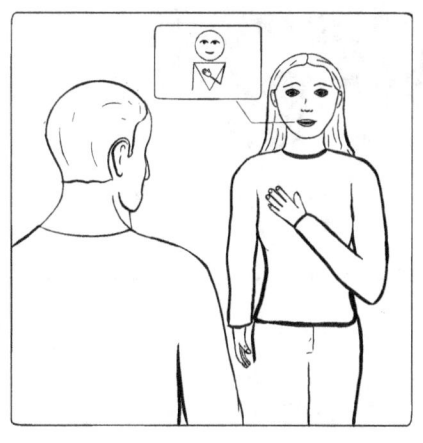
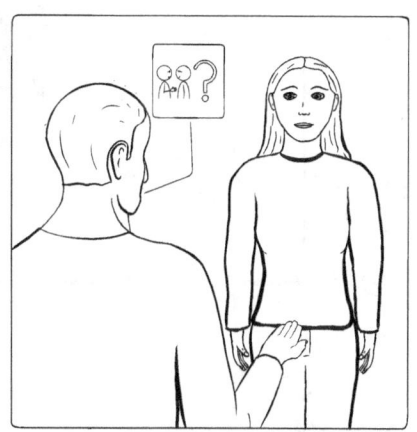
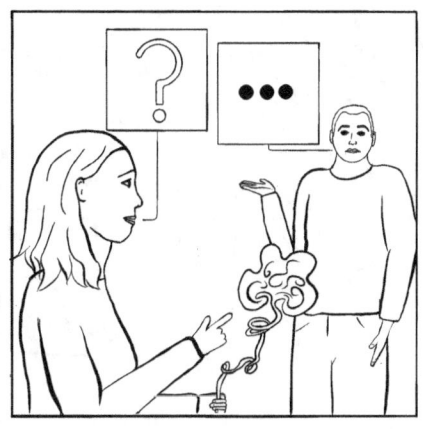
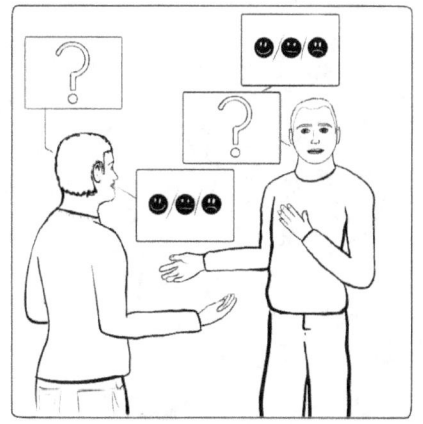
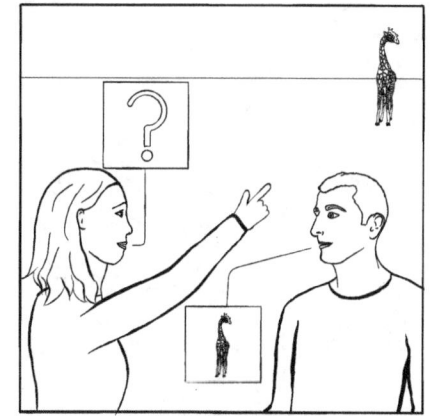

41

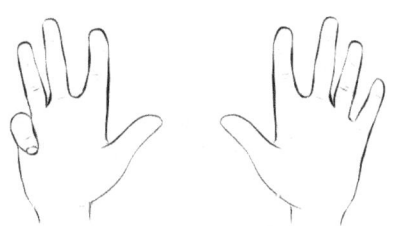

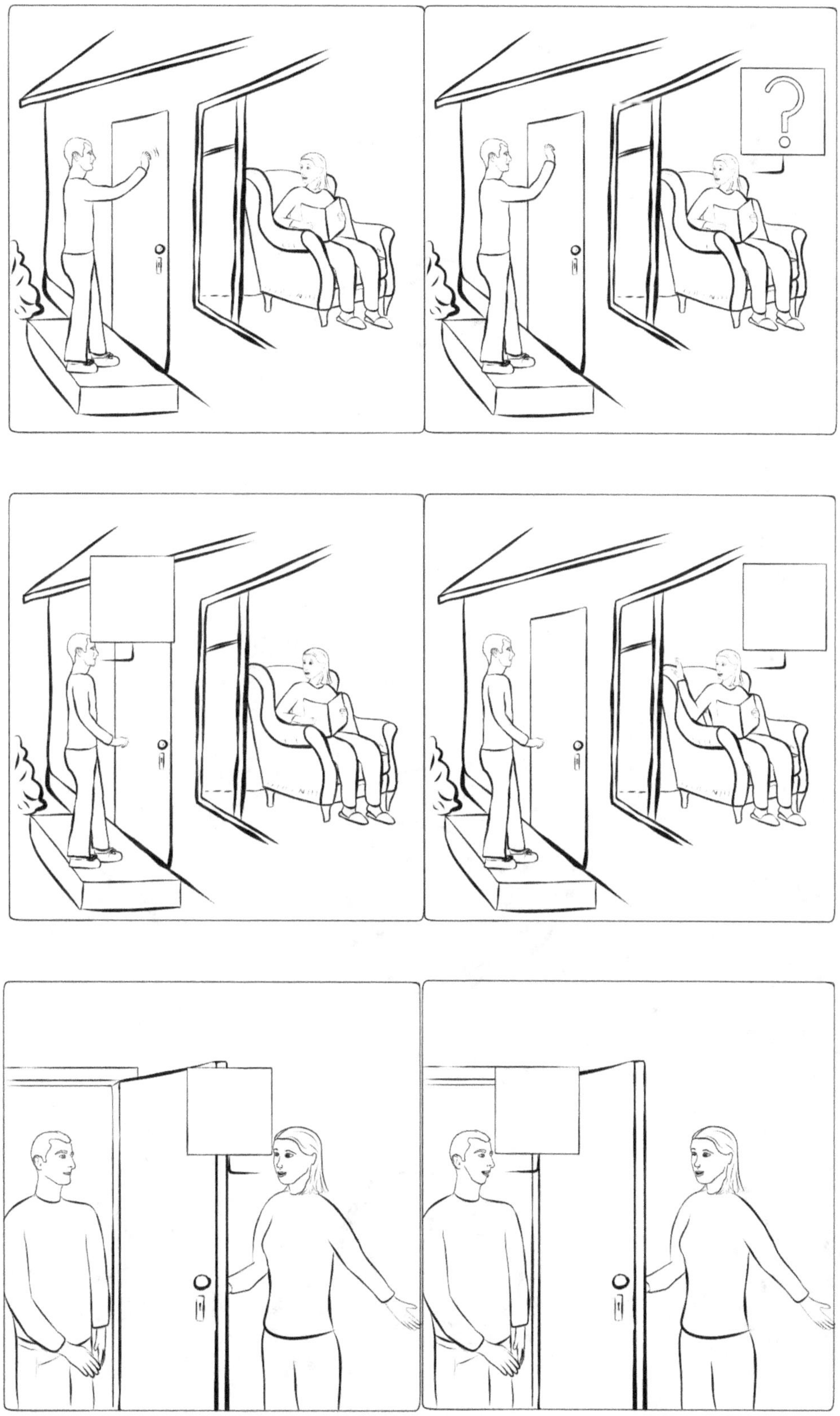

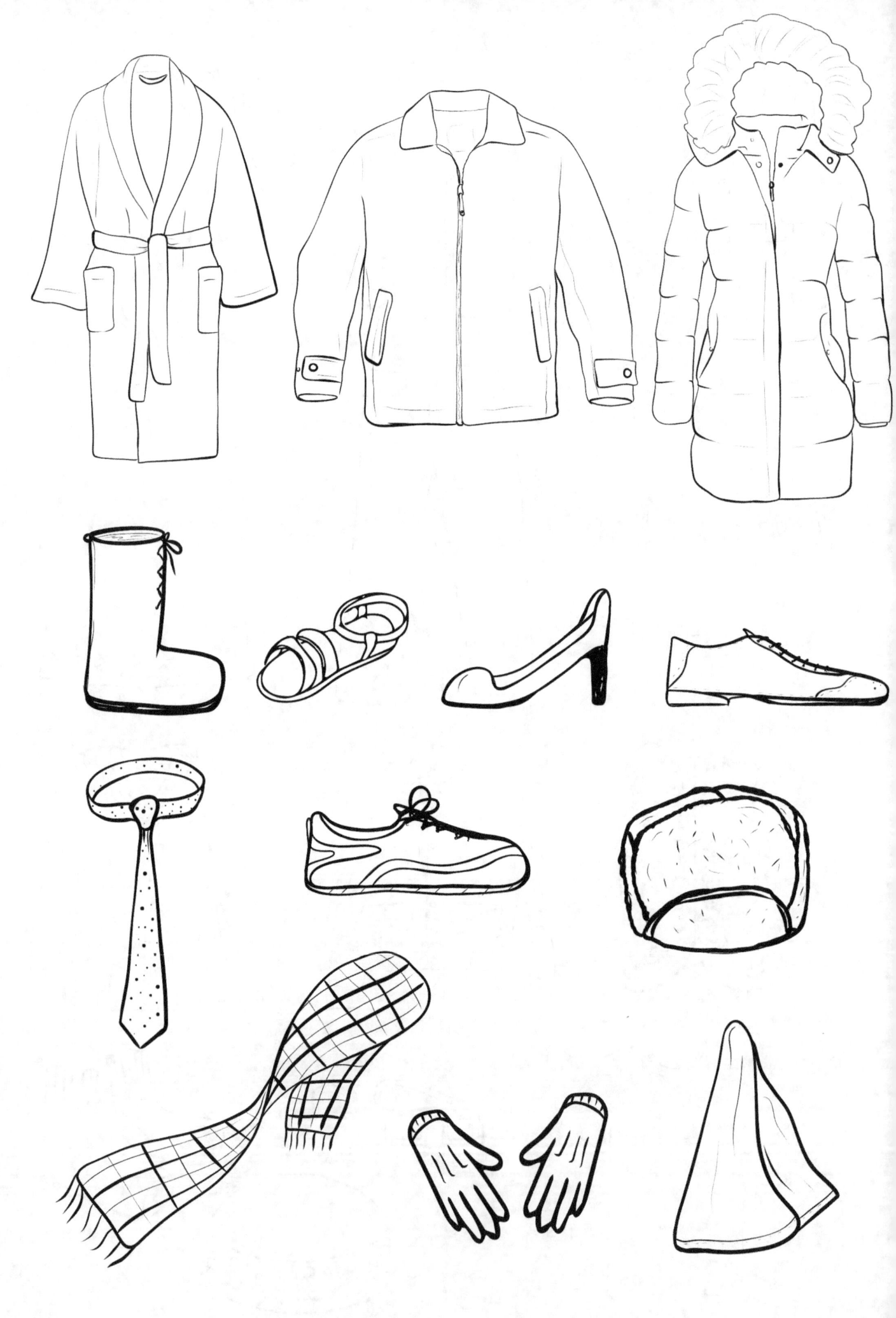

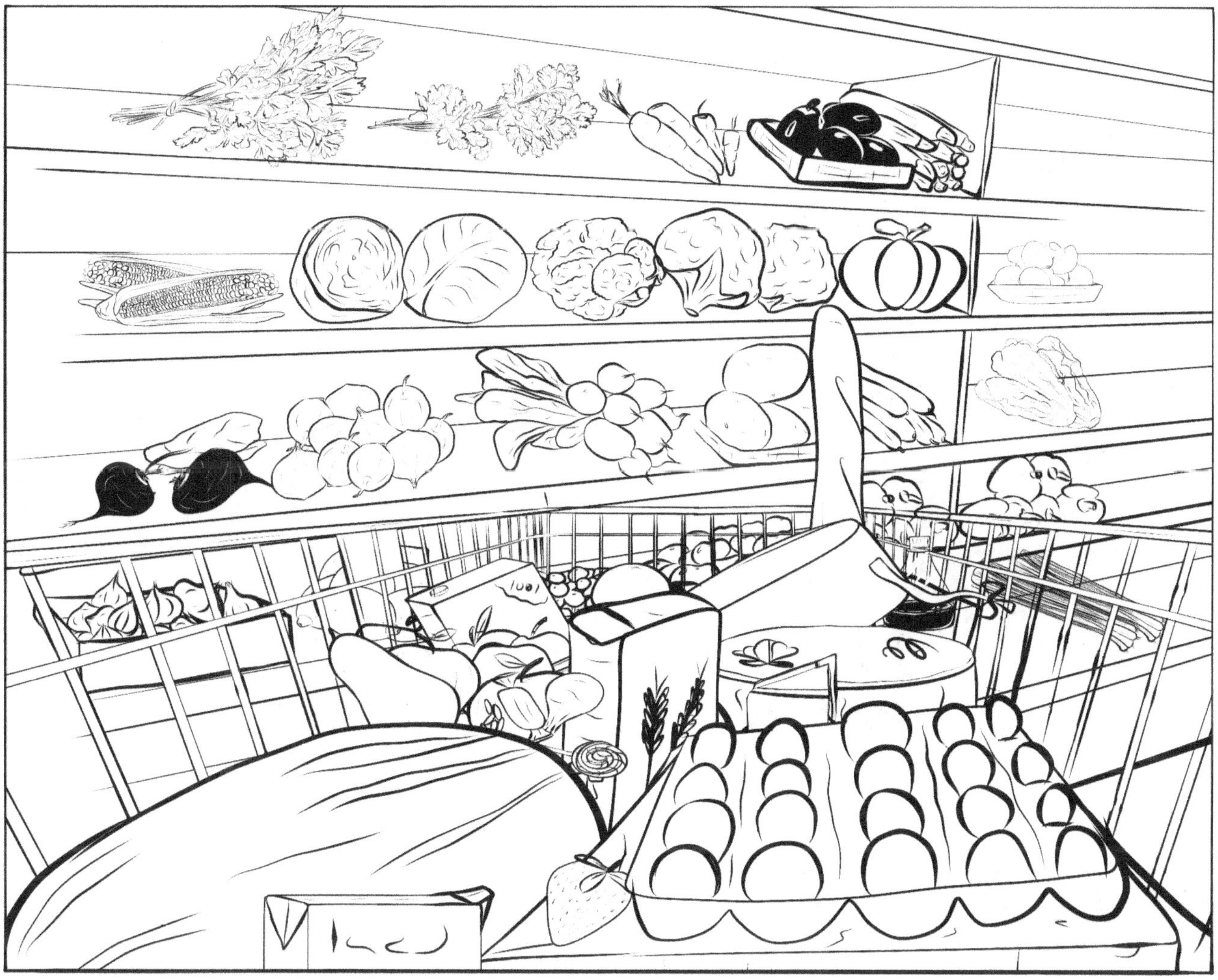

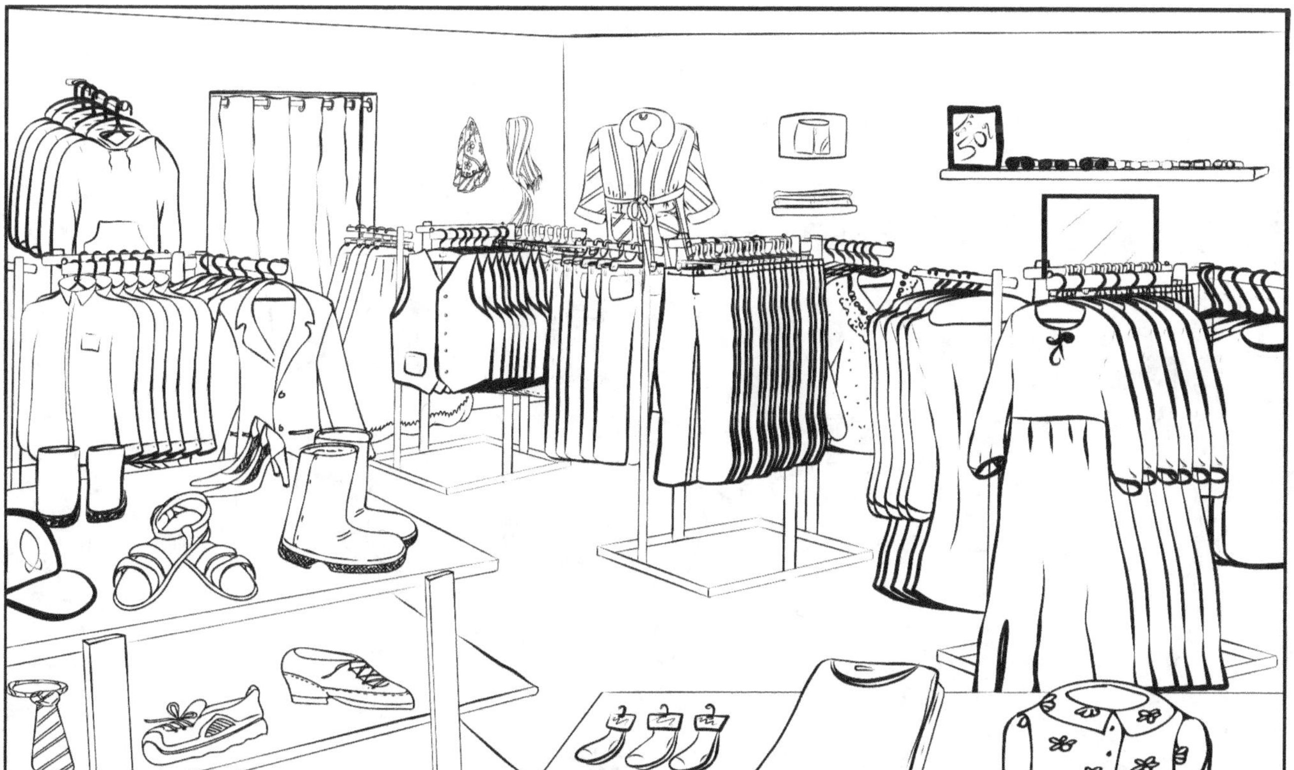

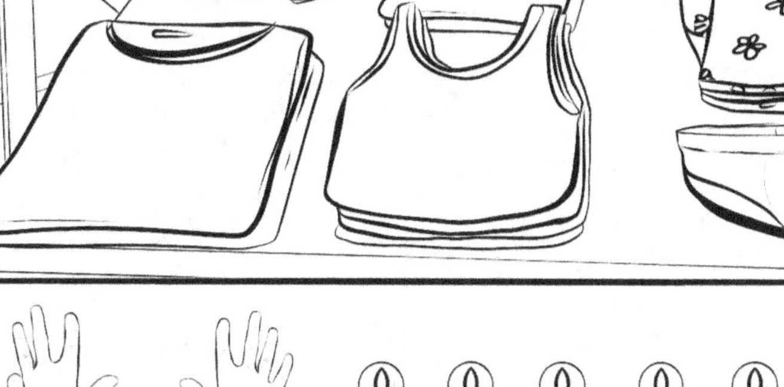

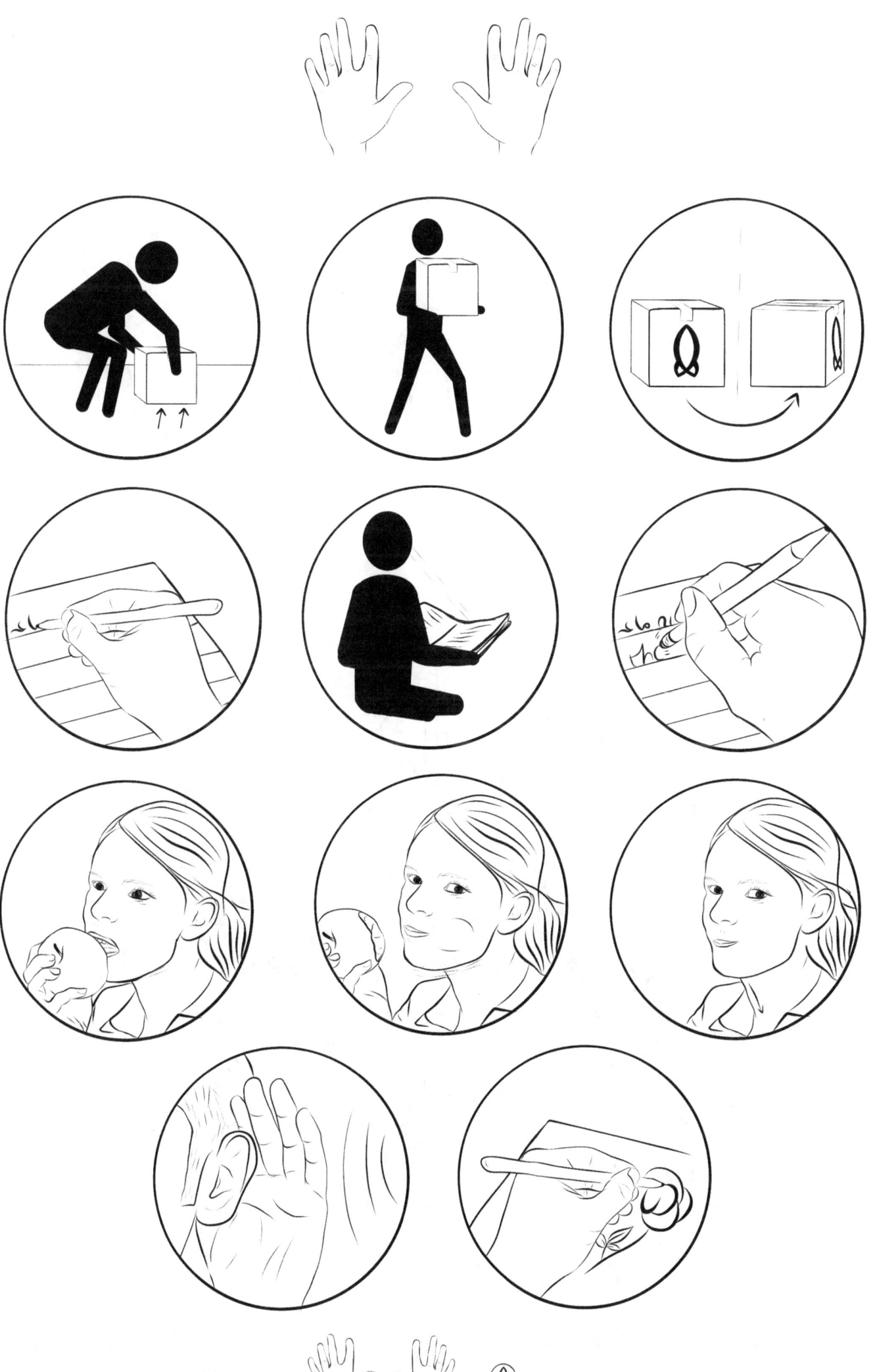

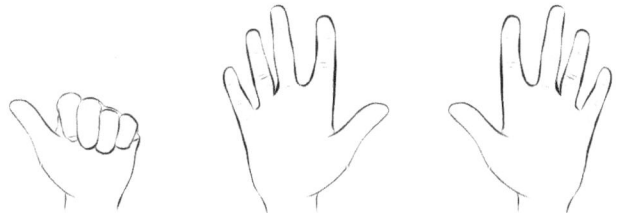

  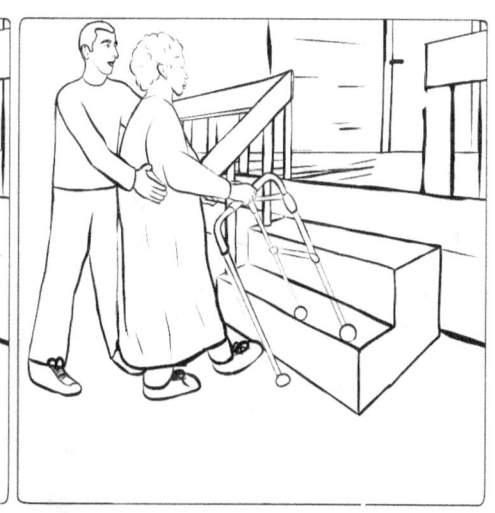

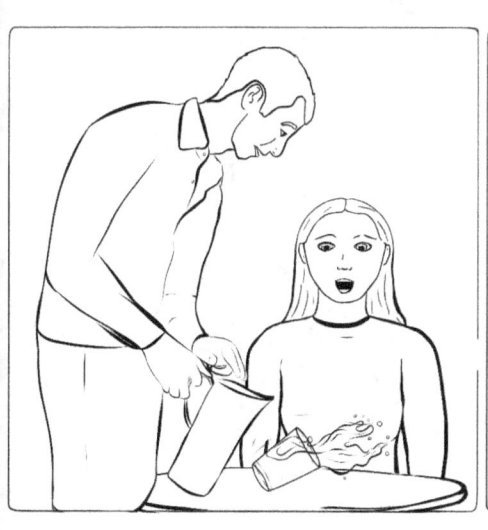 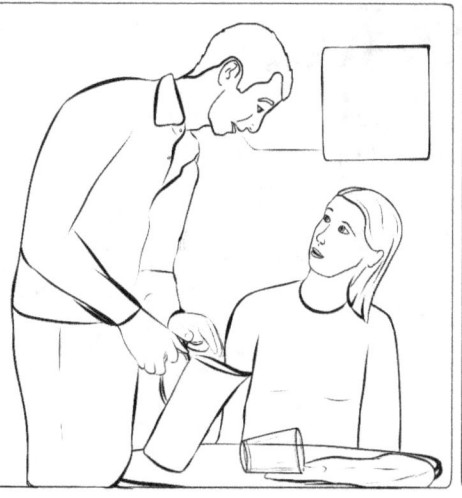 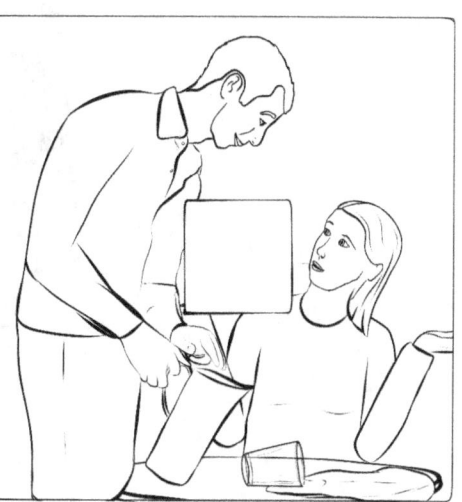

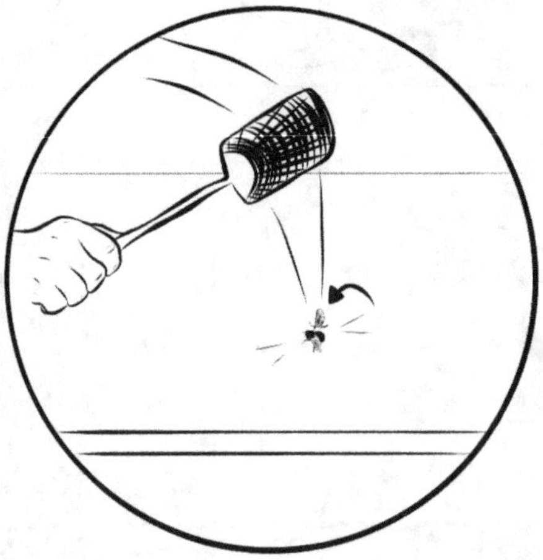

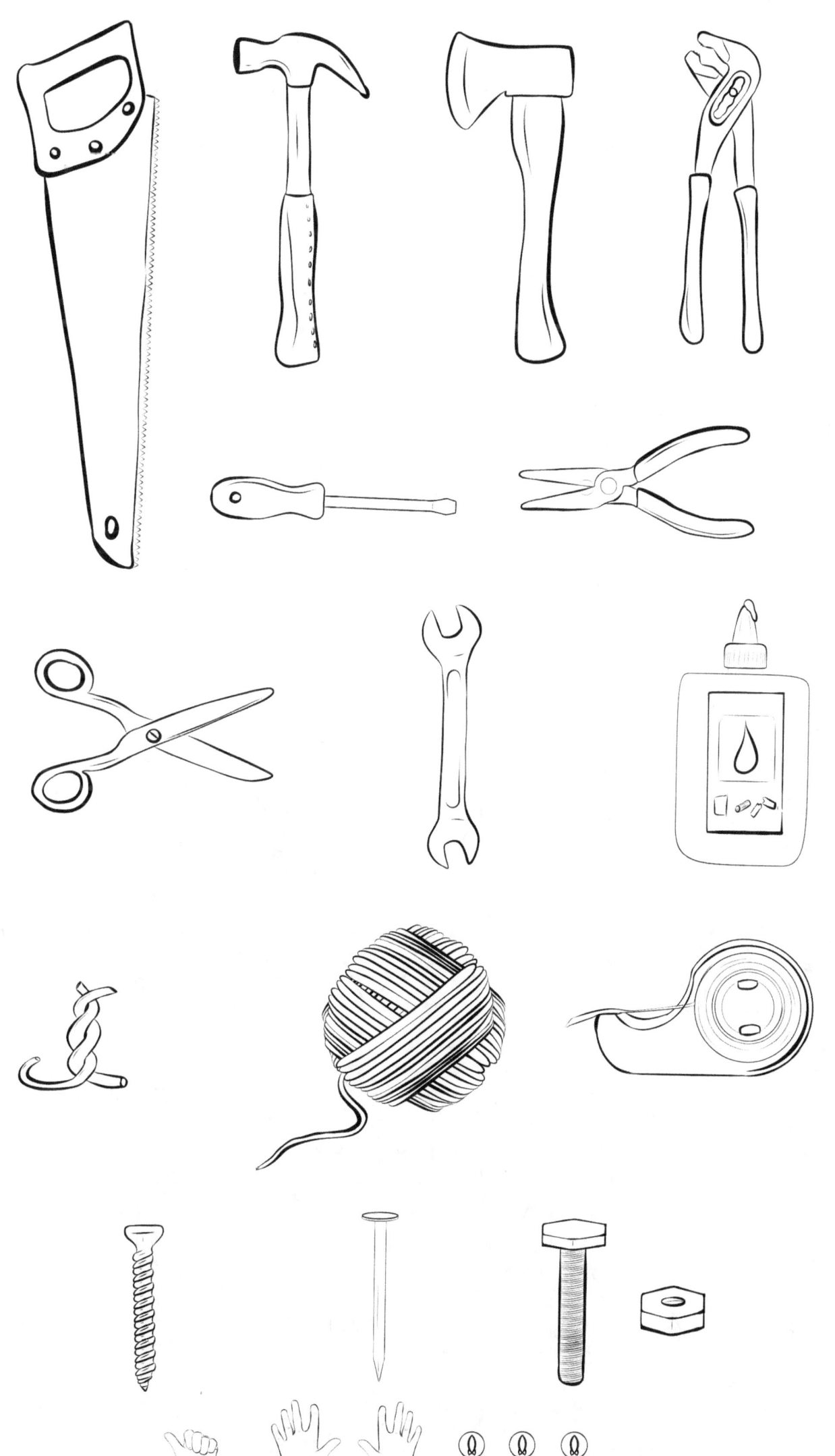

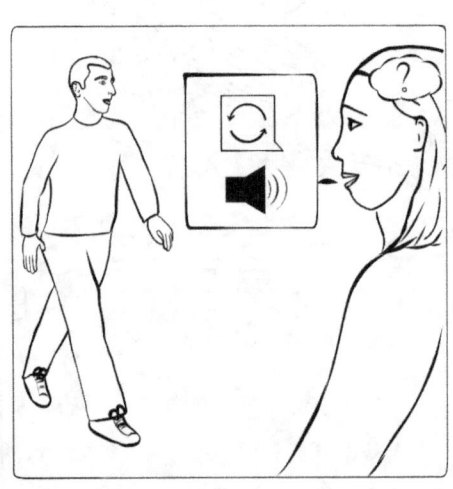
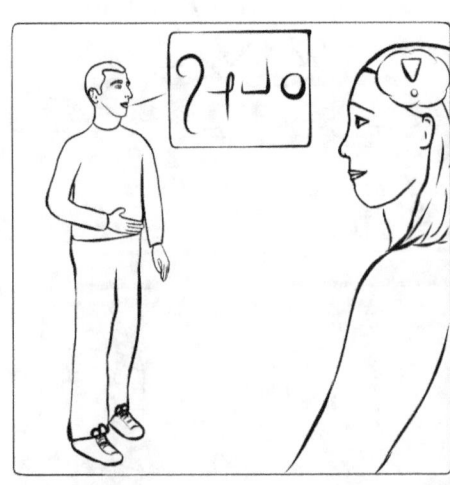

62

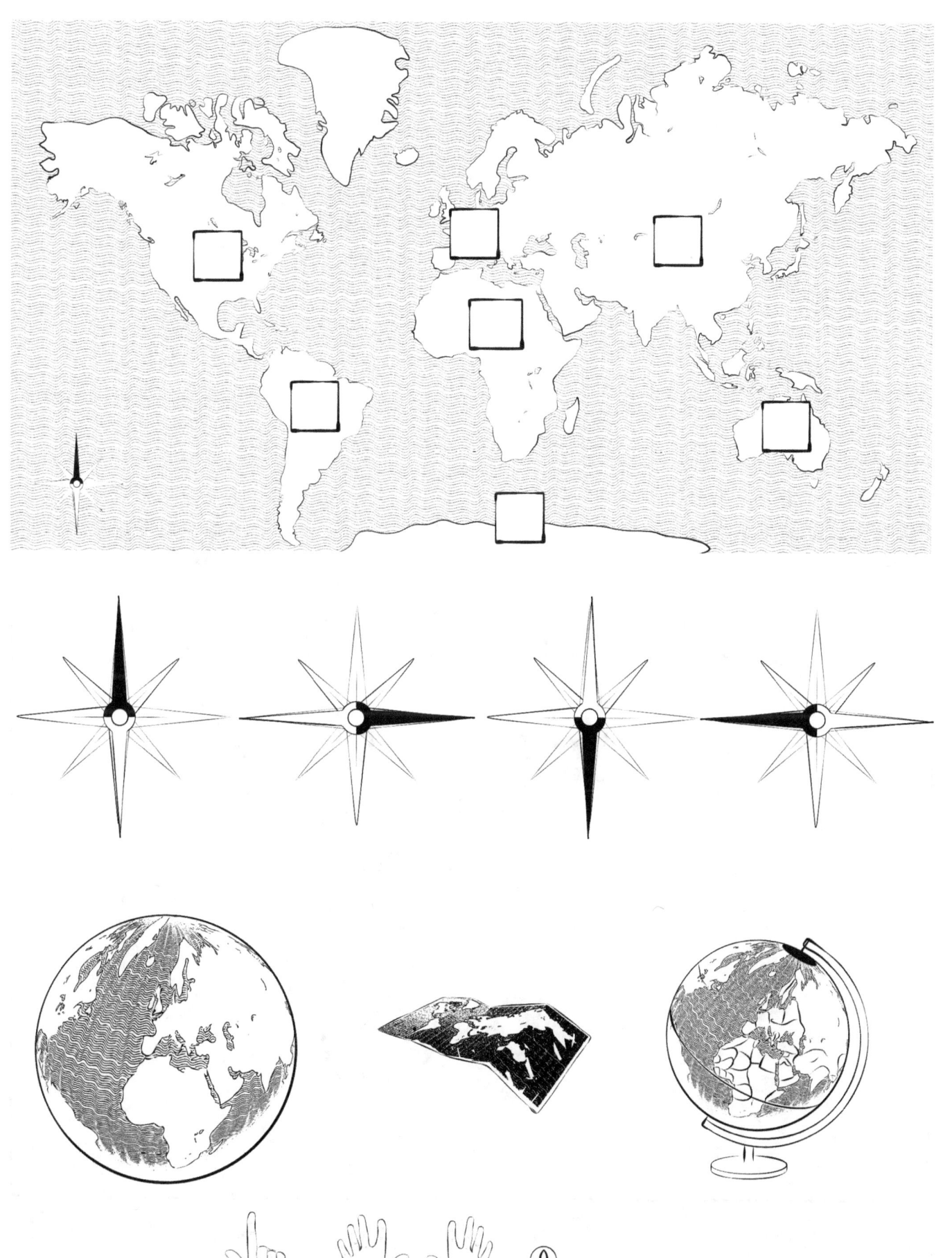

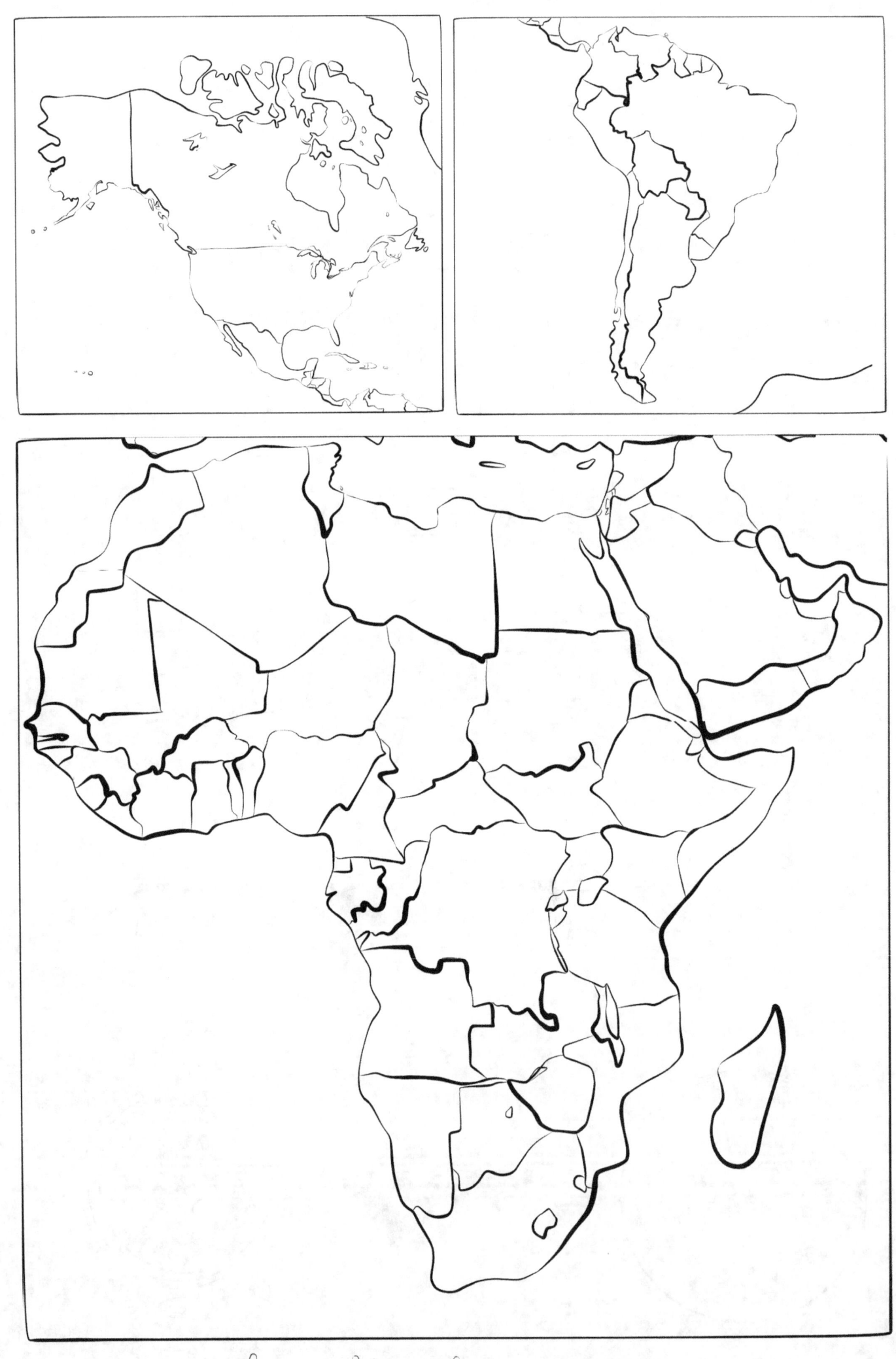

66

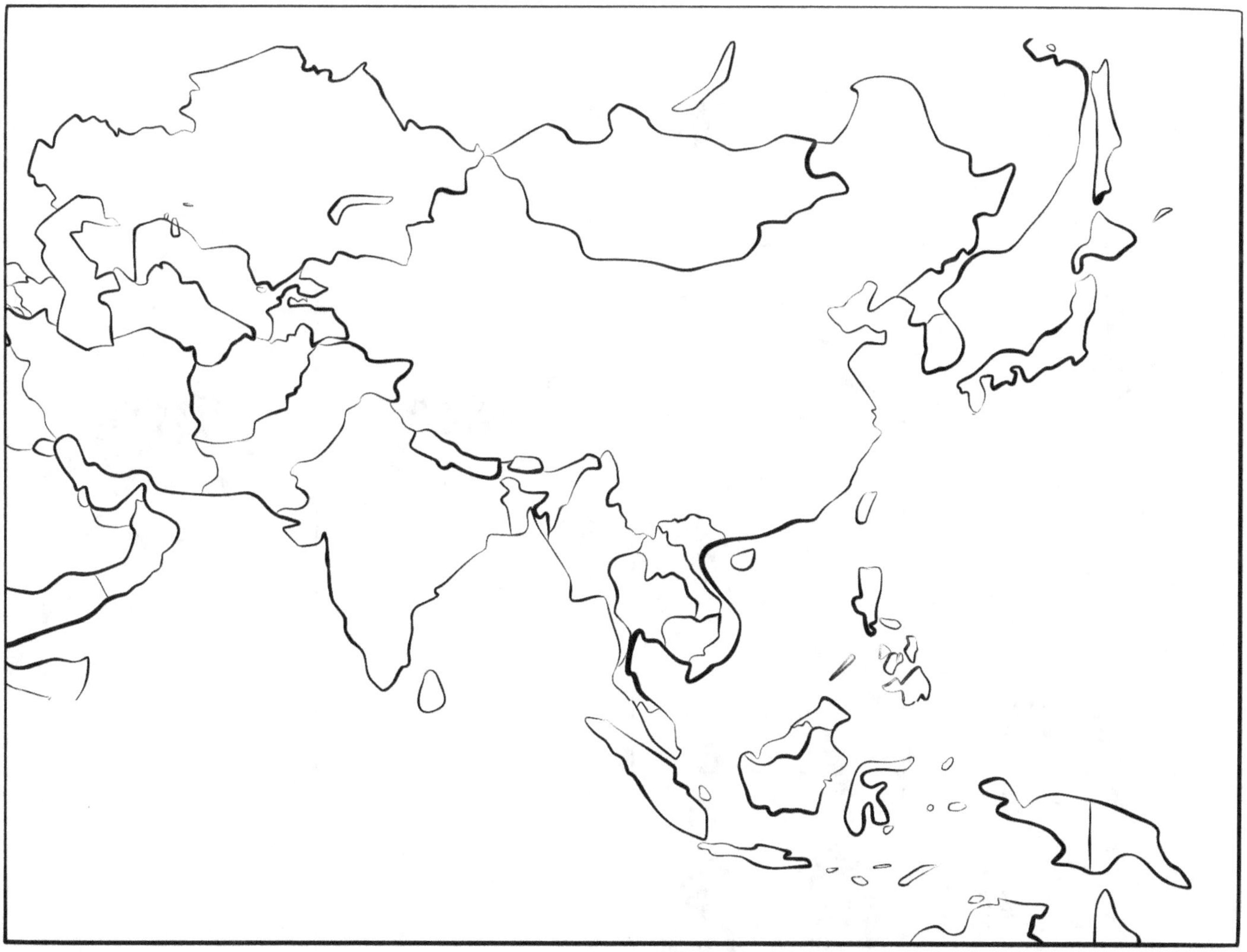

69

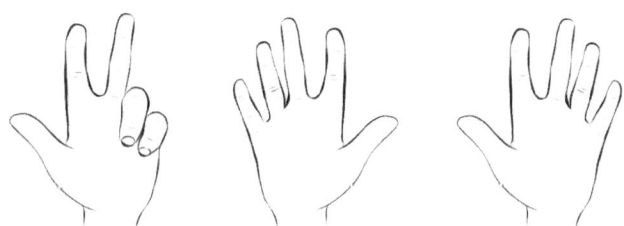

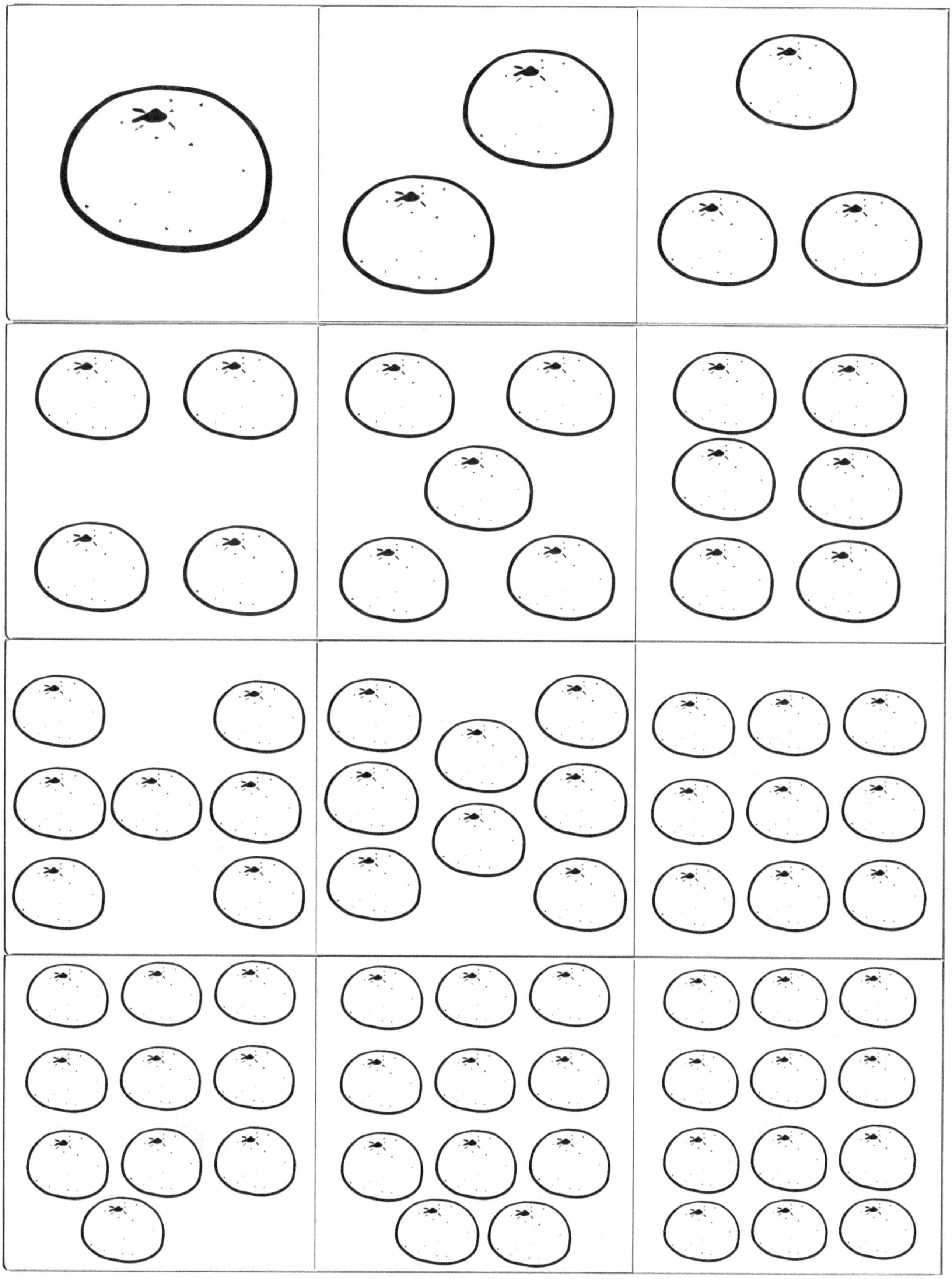

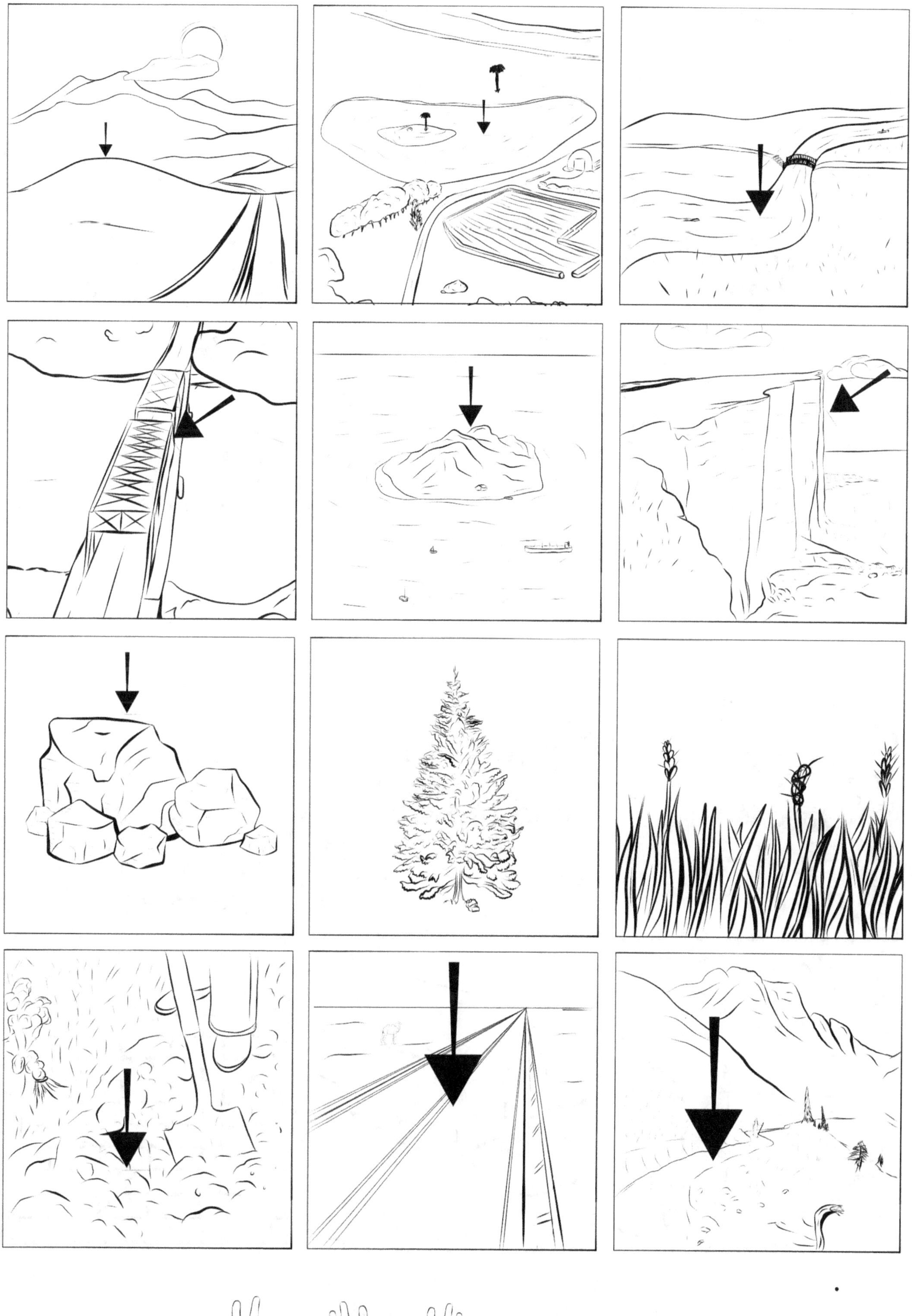

73

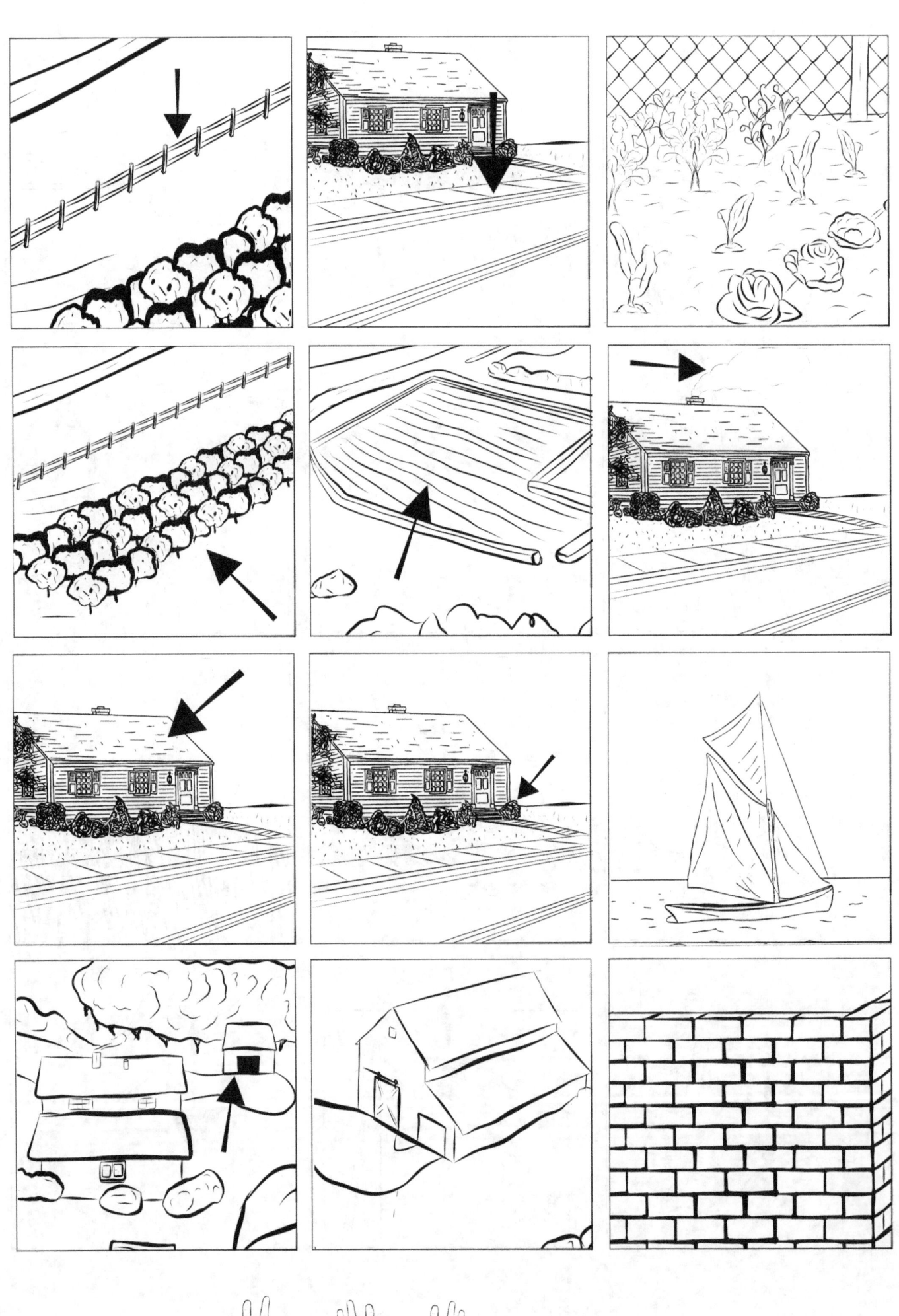

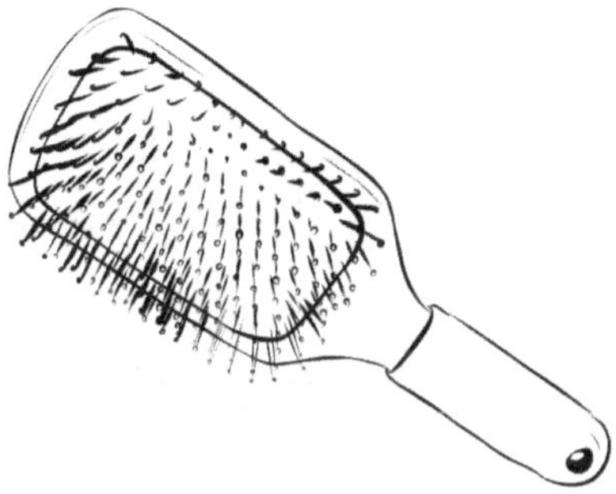

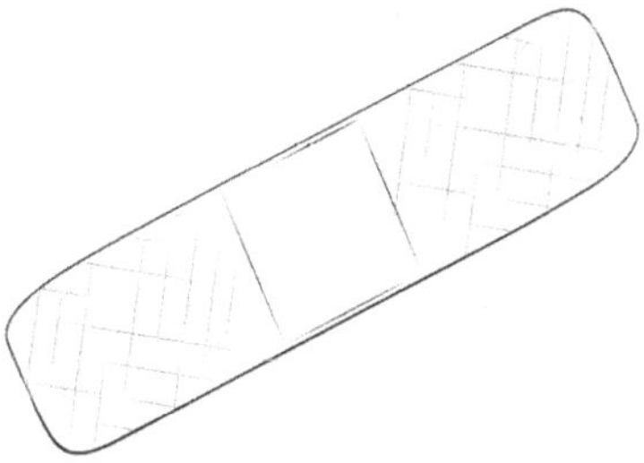

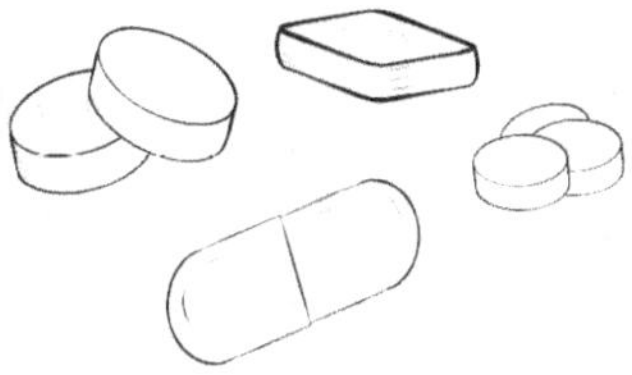

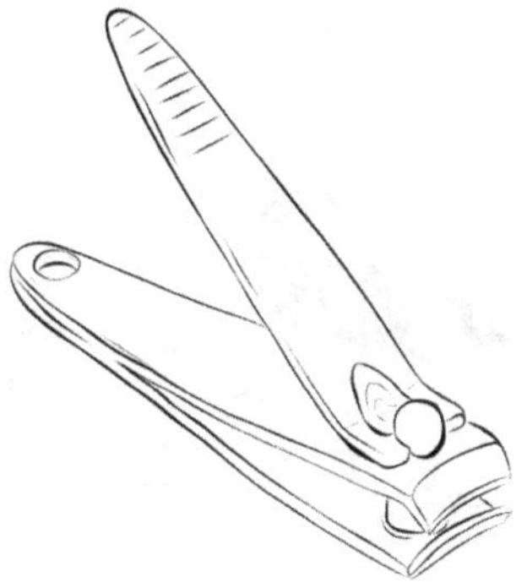

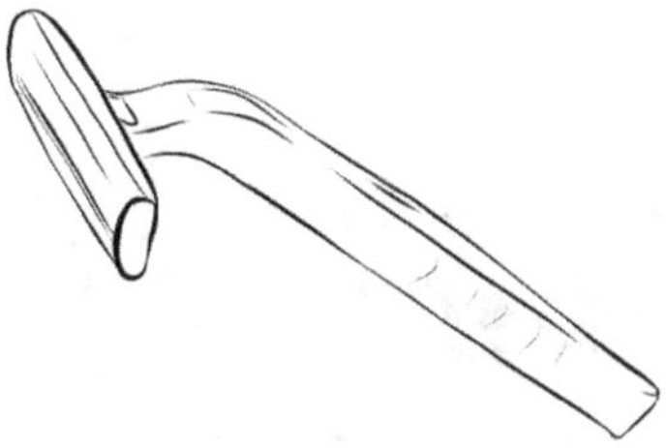

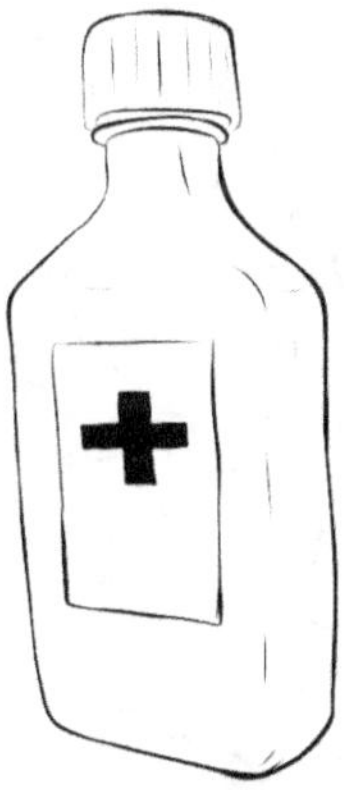

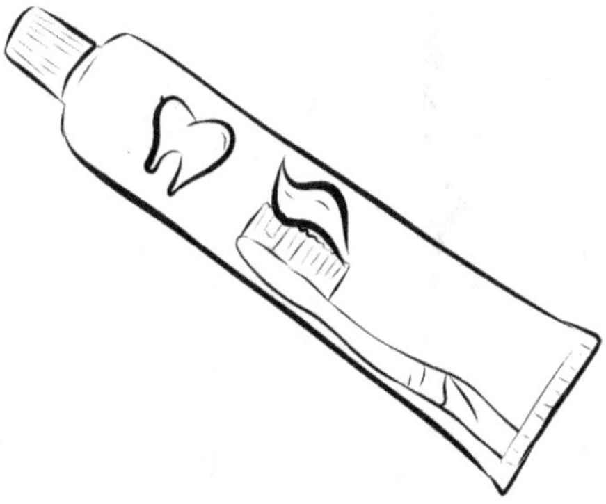

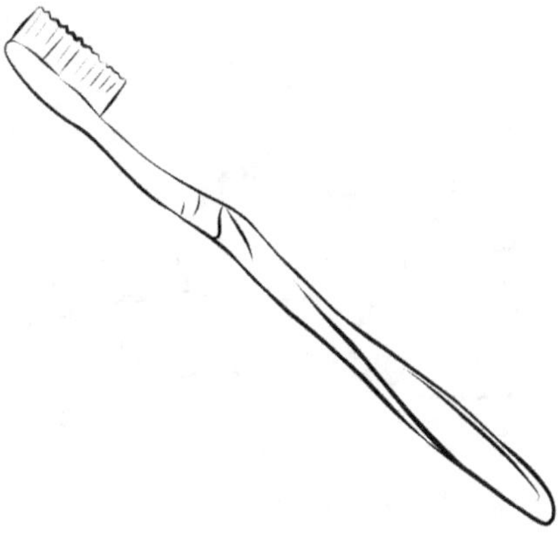

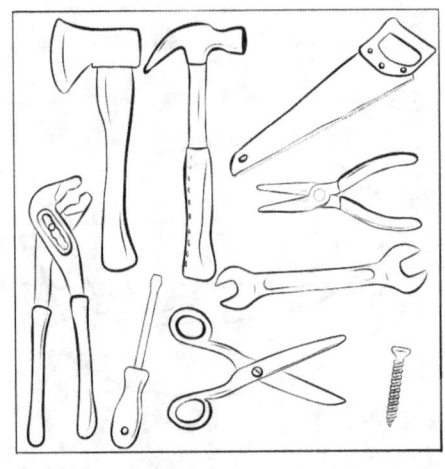

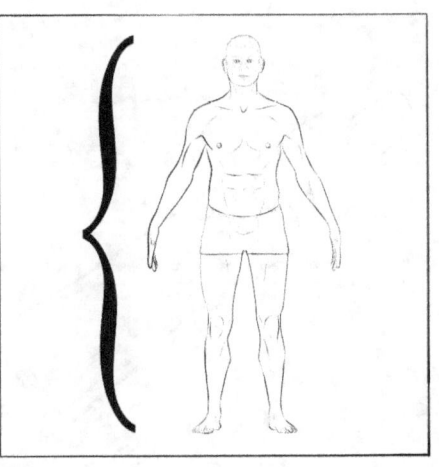

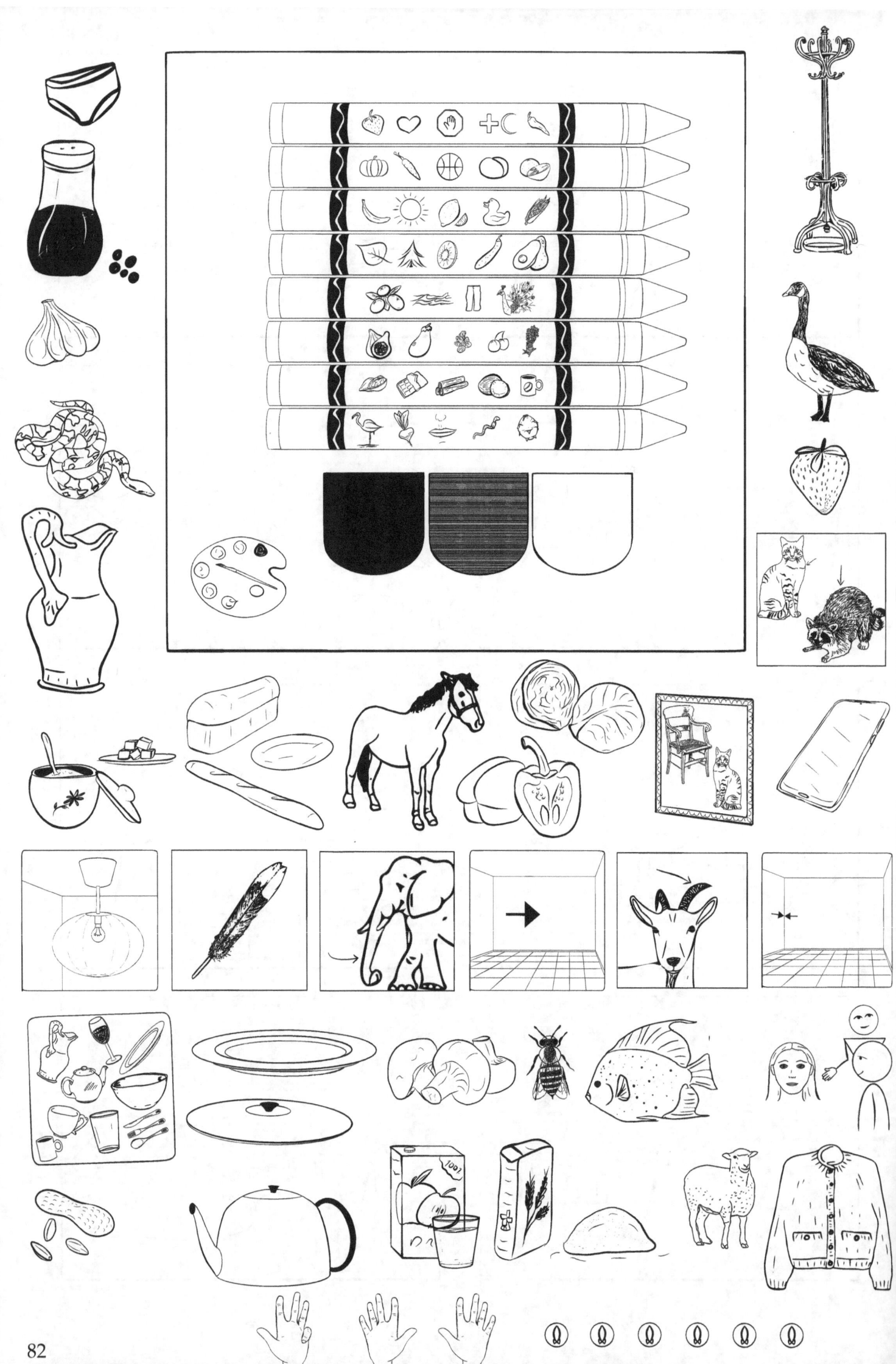

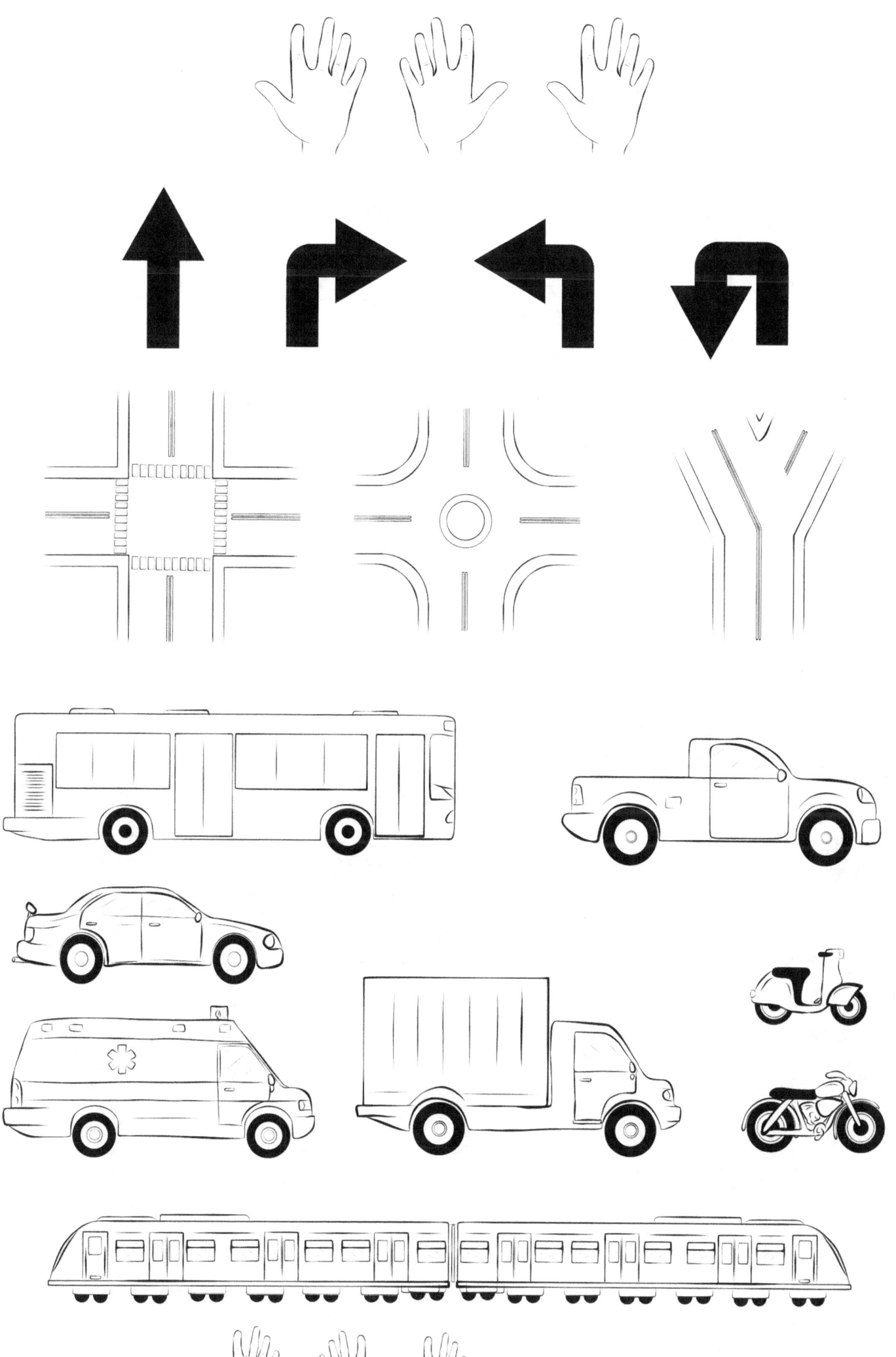

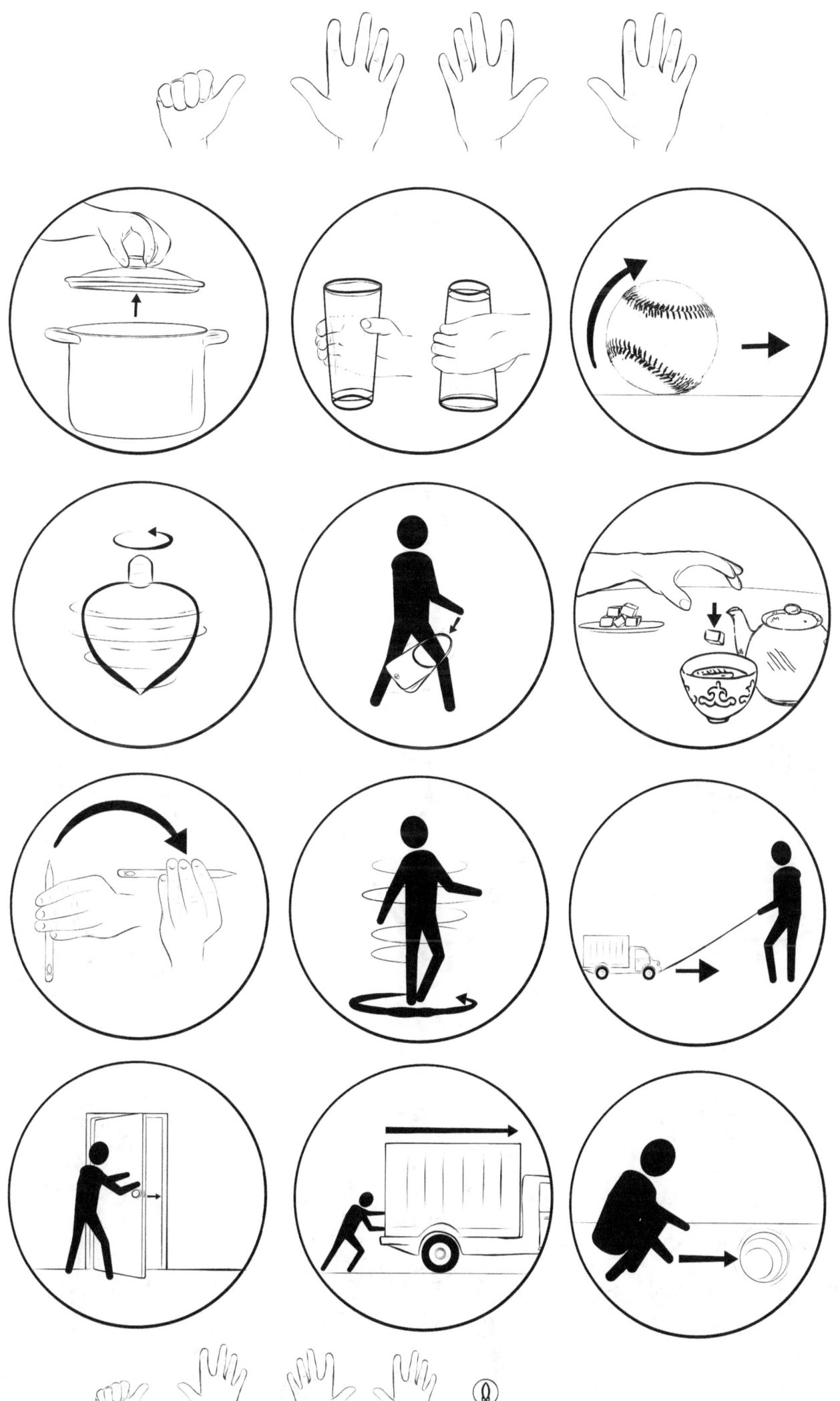

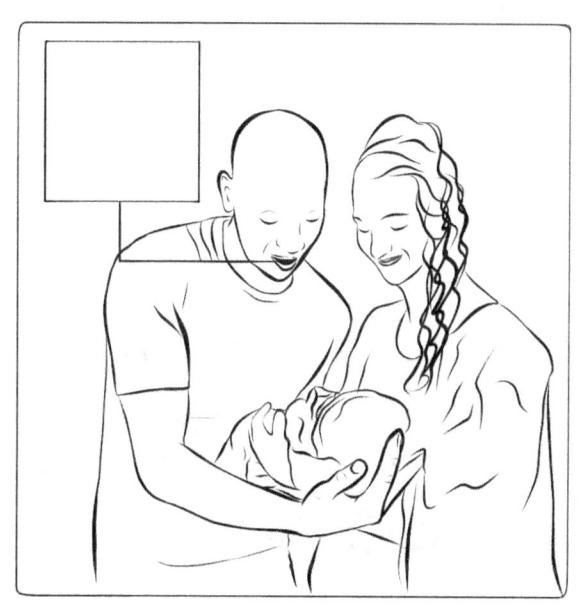

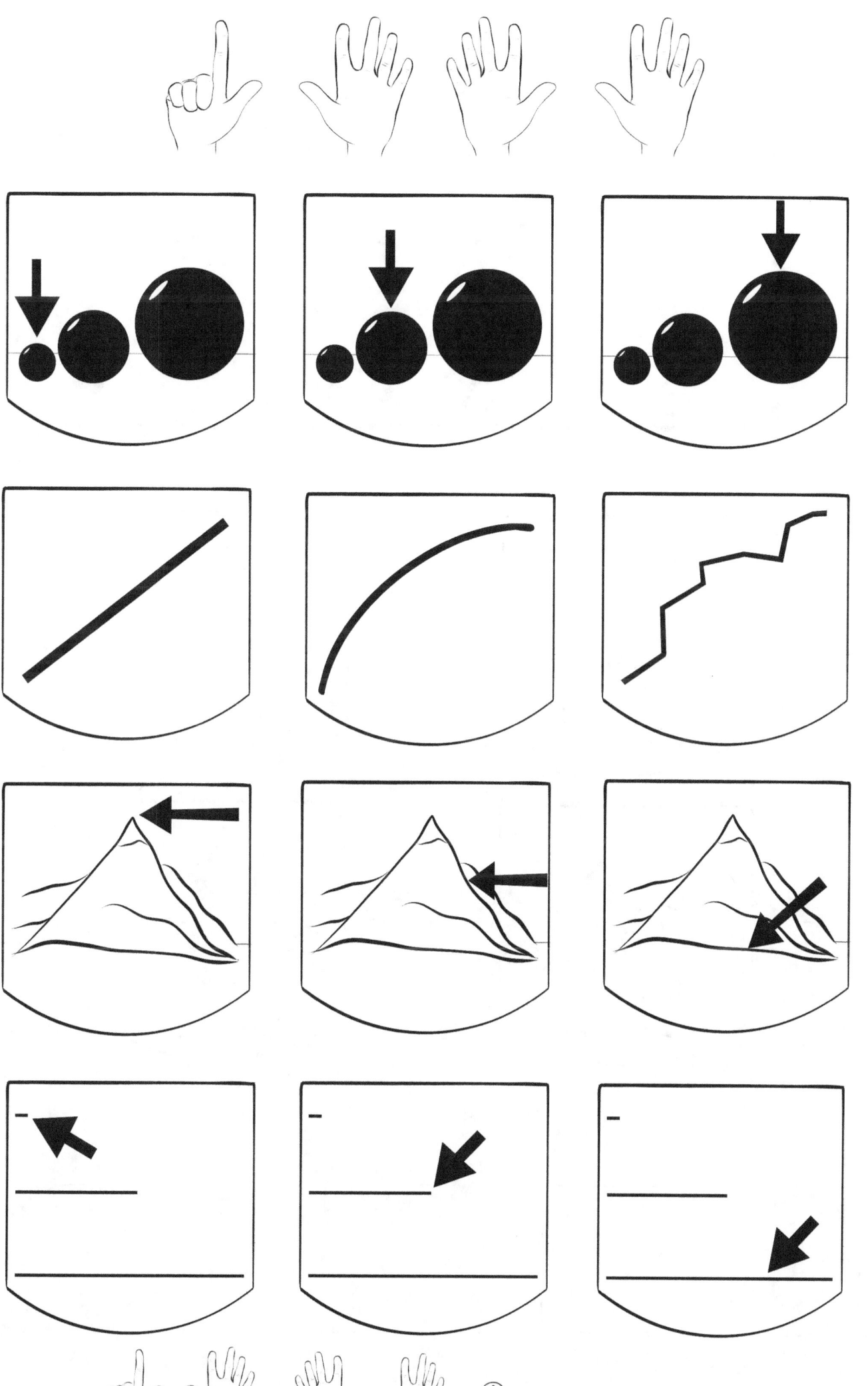

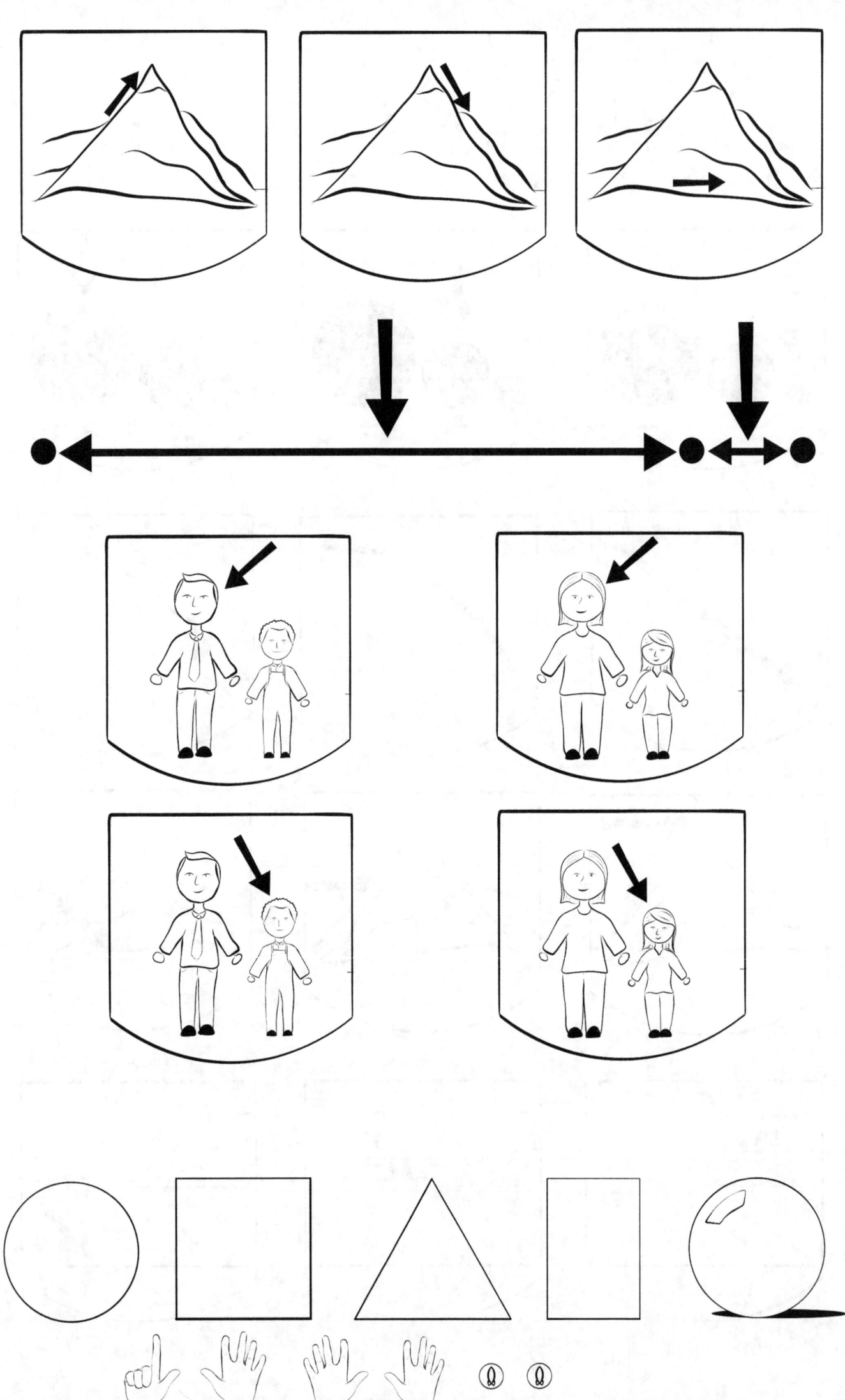

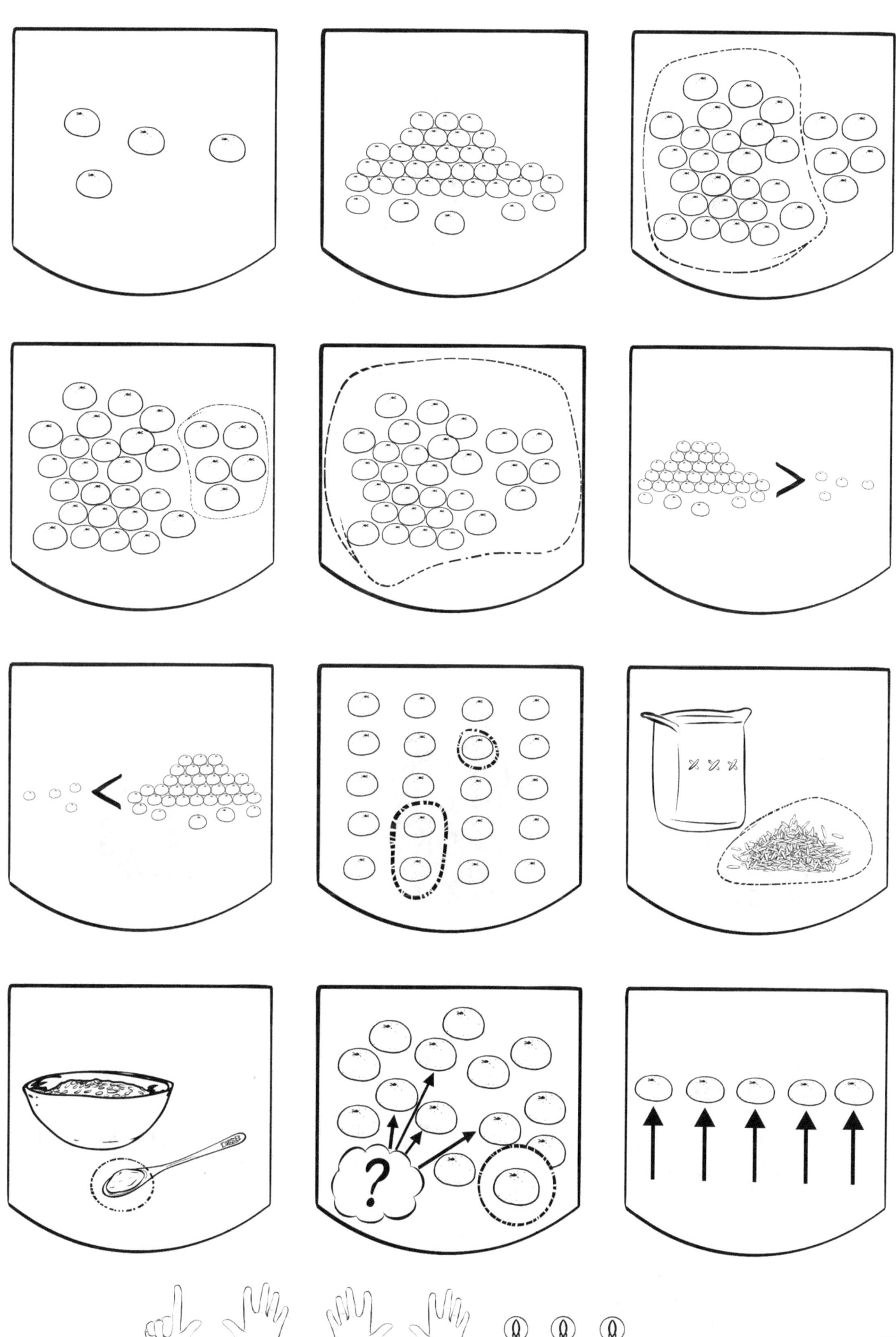

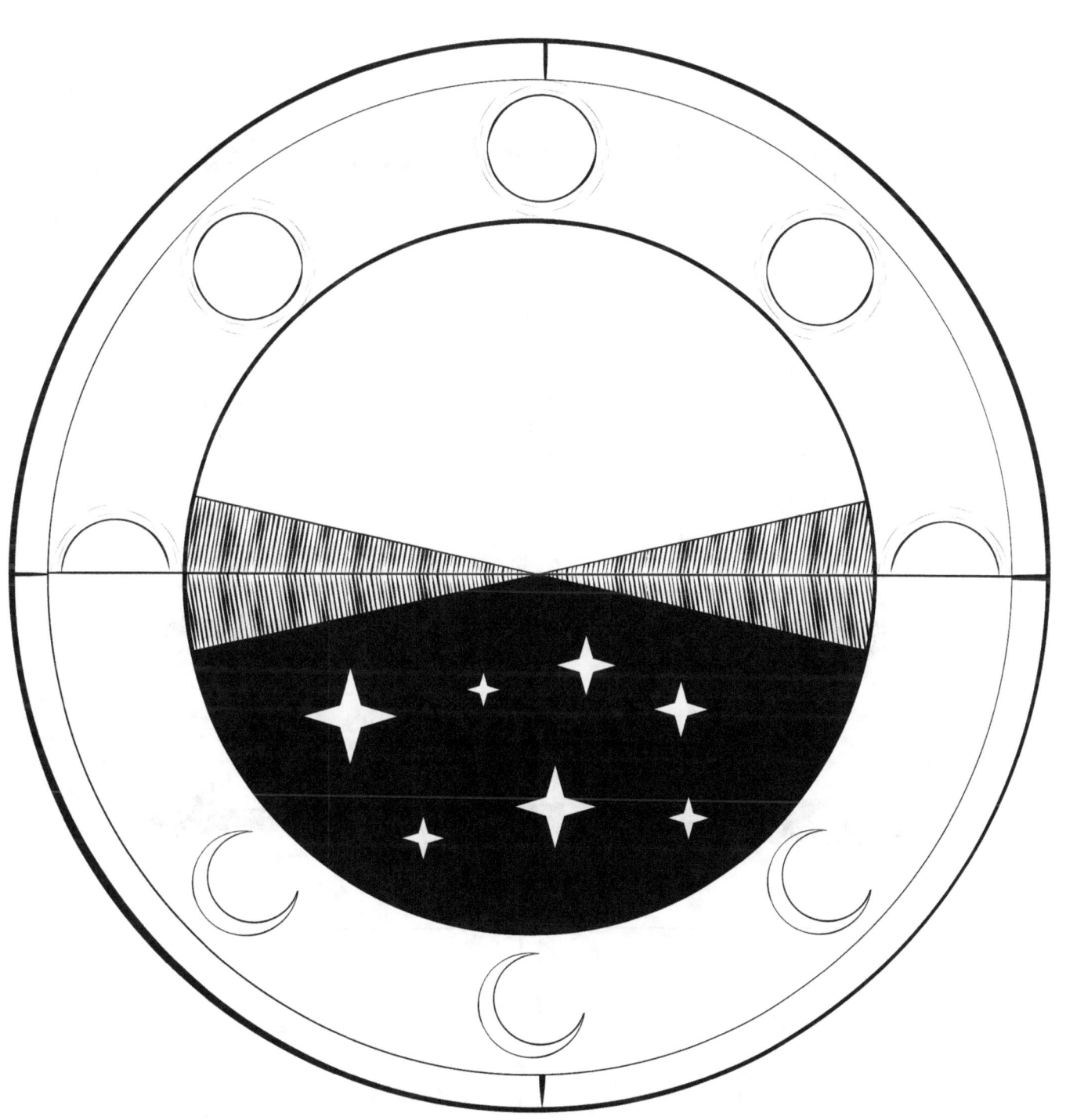

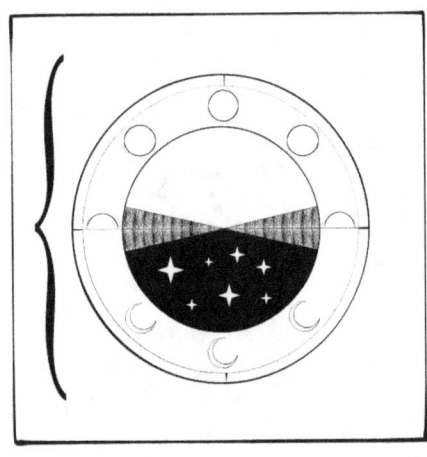
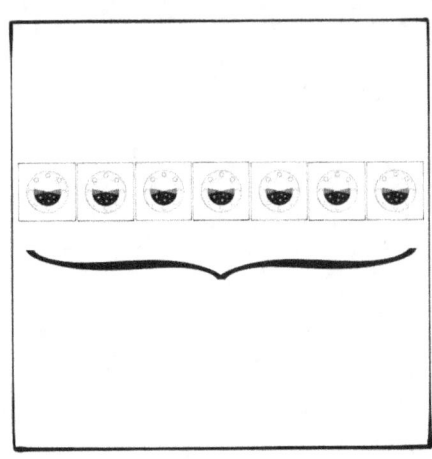

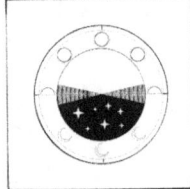 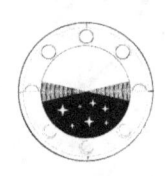 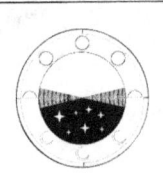 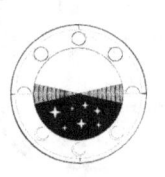 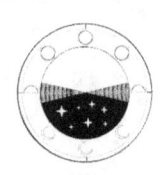 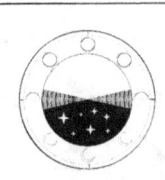 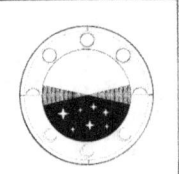

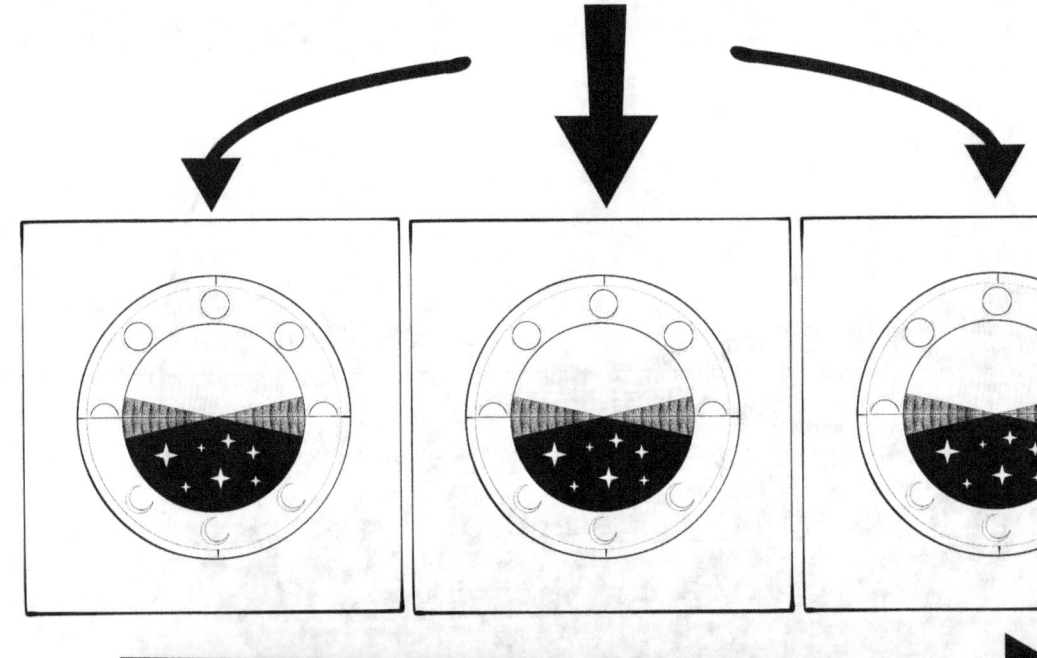

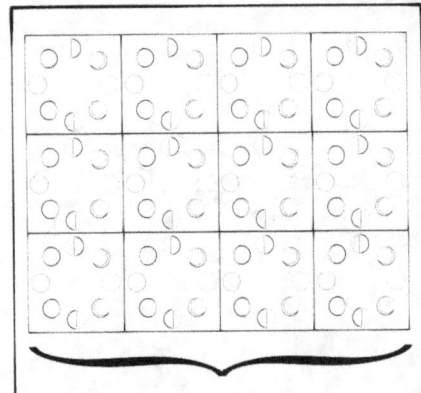
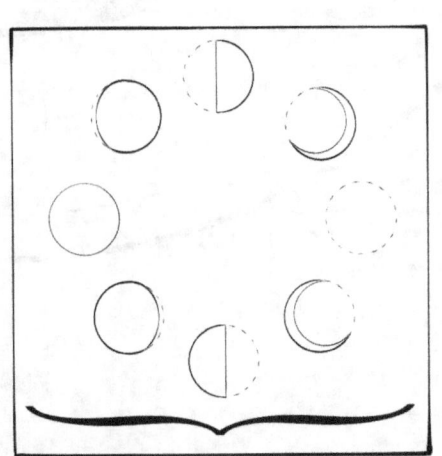

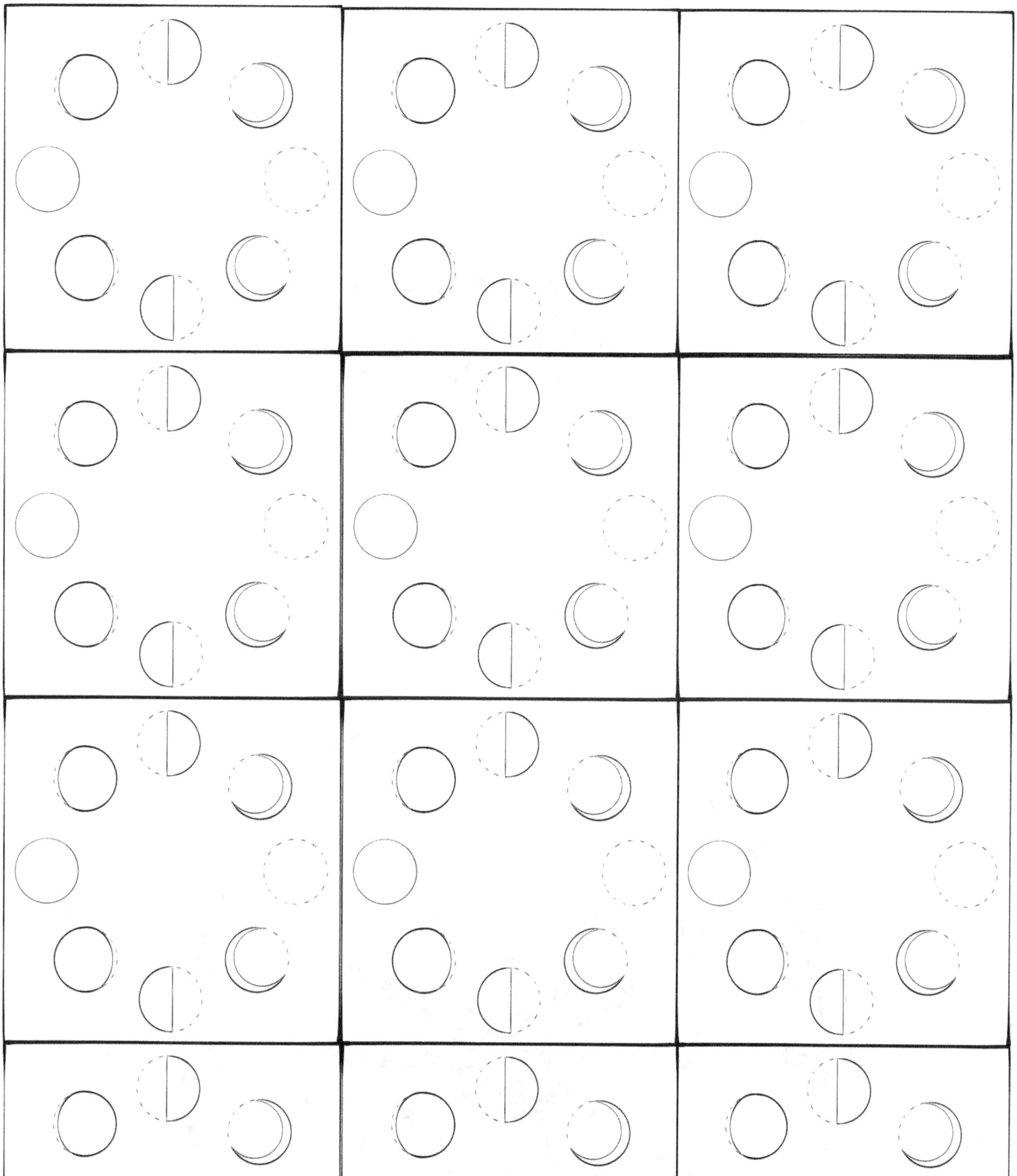

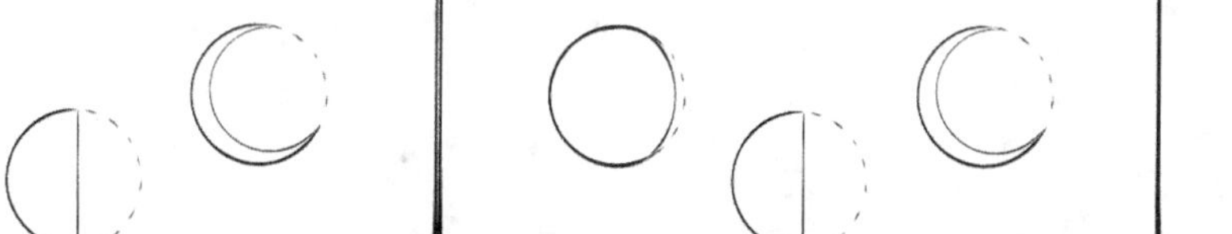

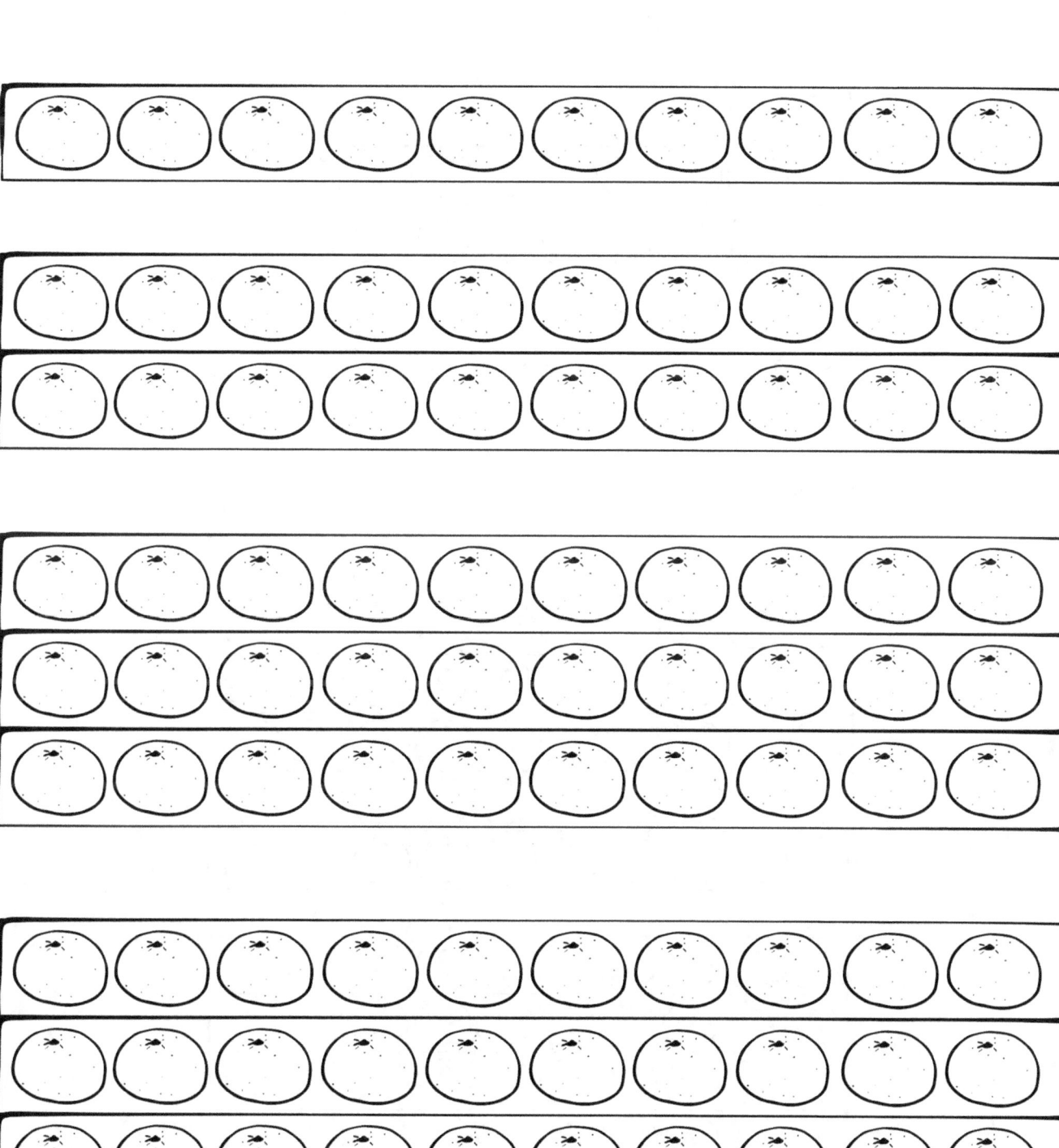

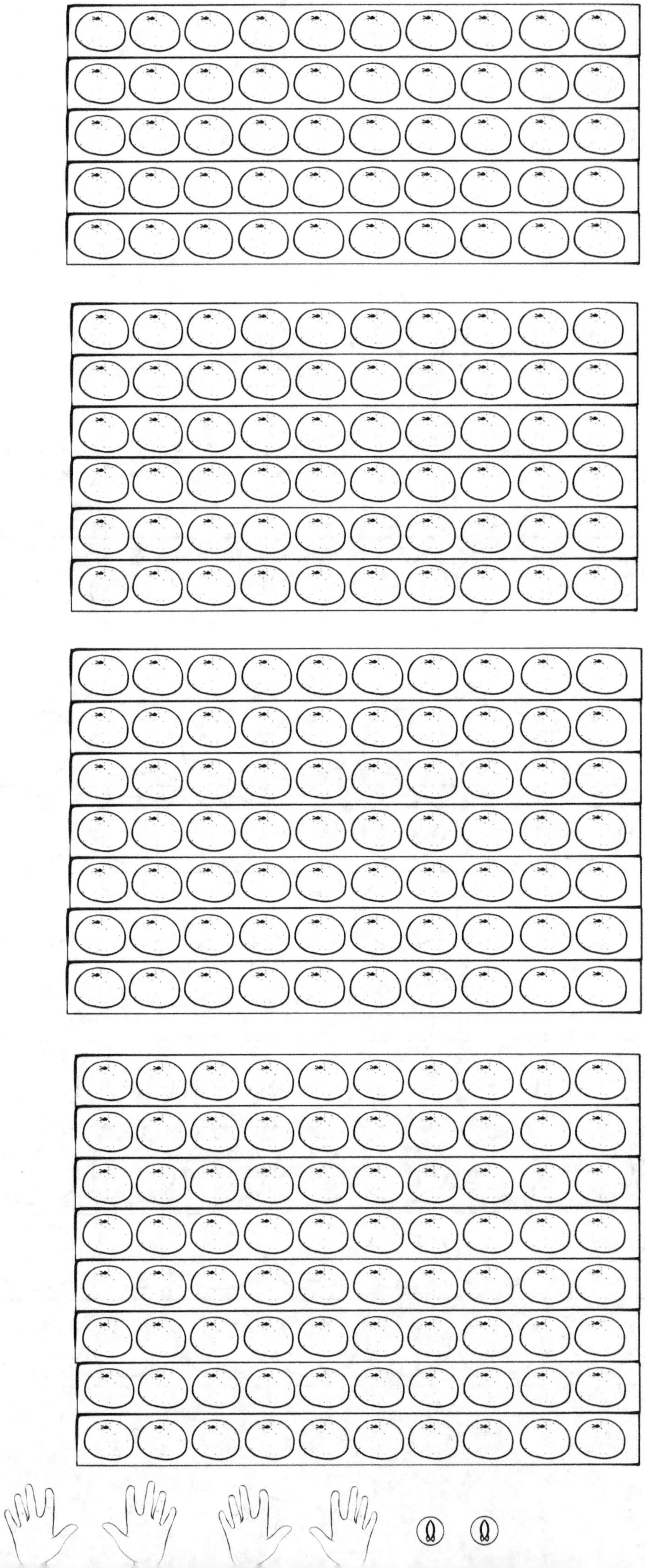

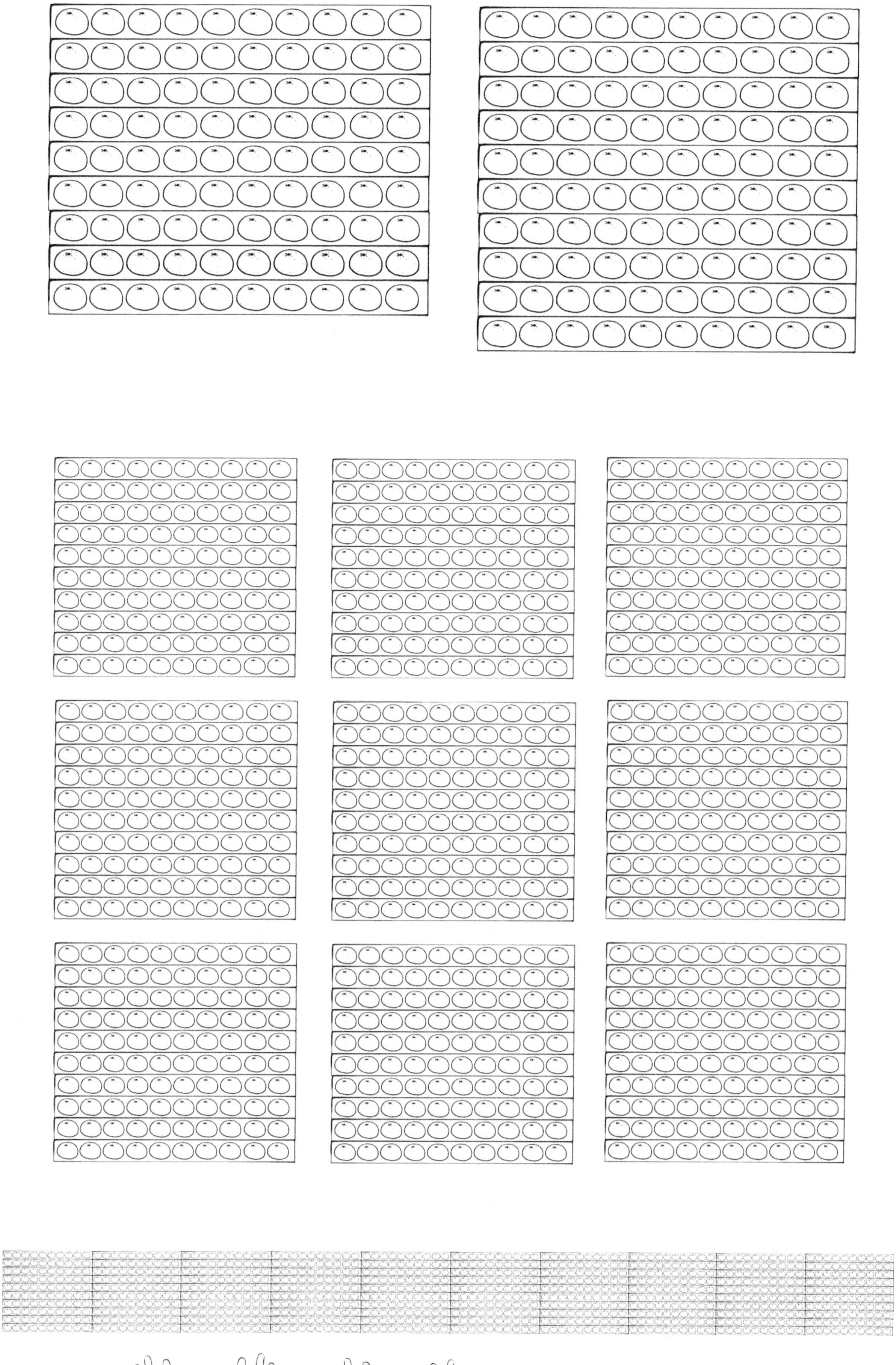

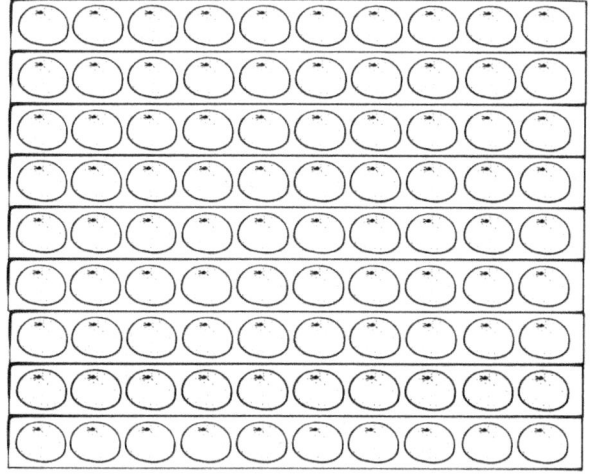
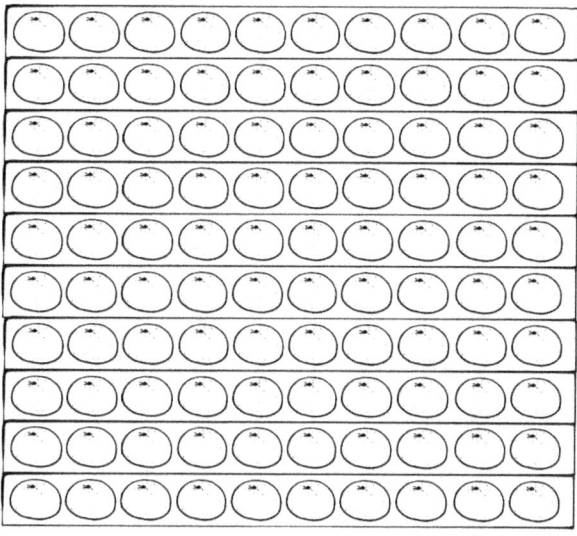

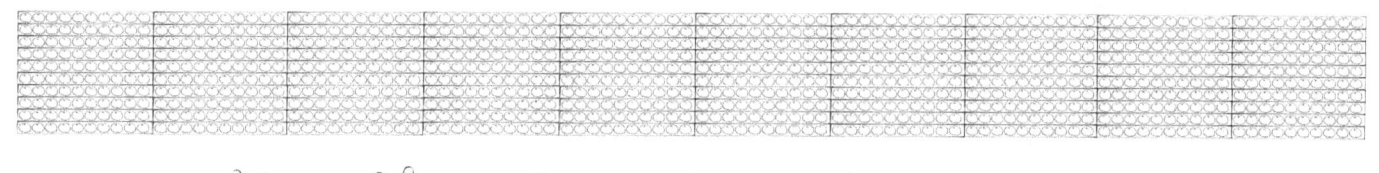

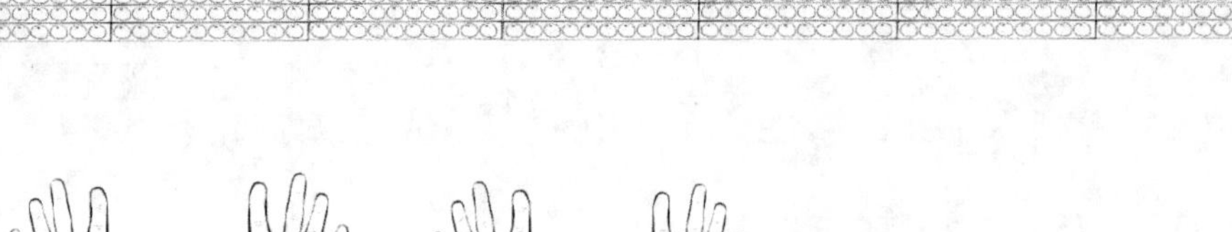

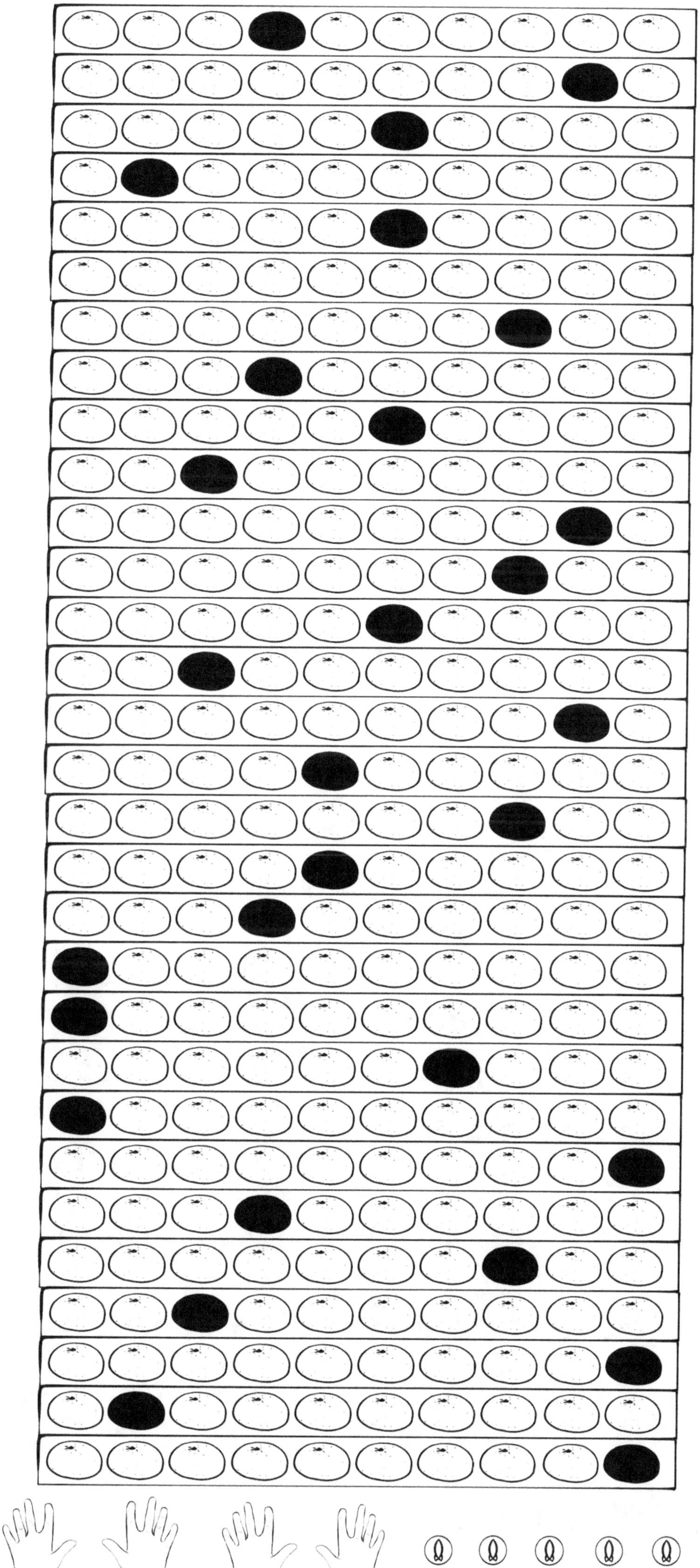

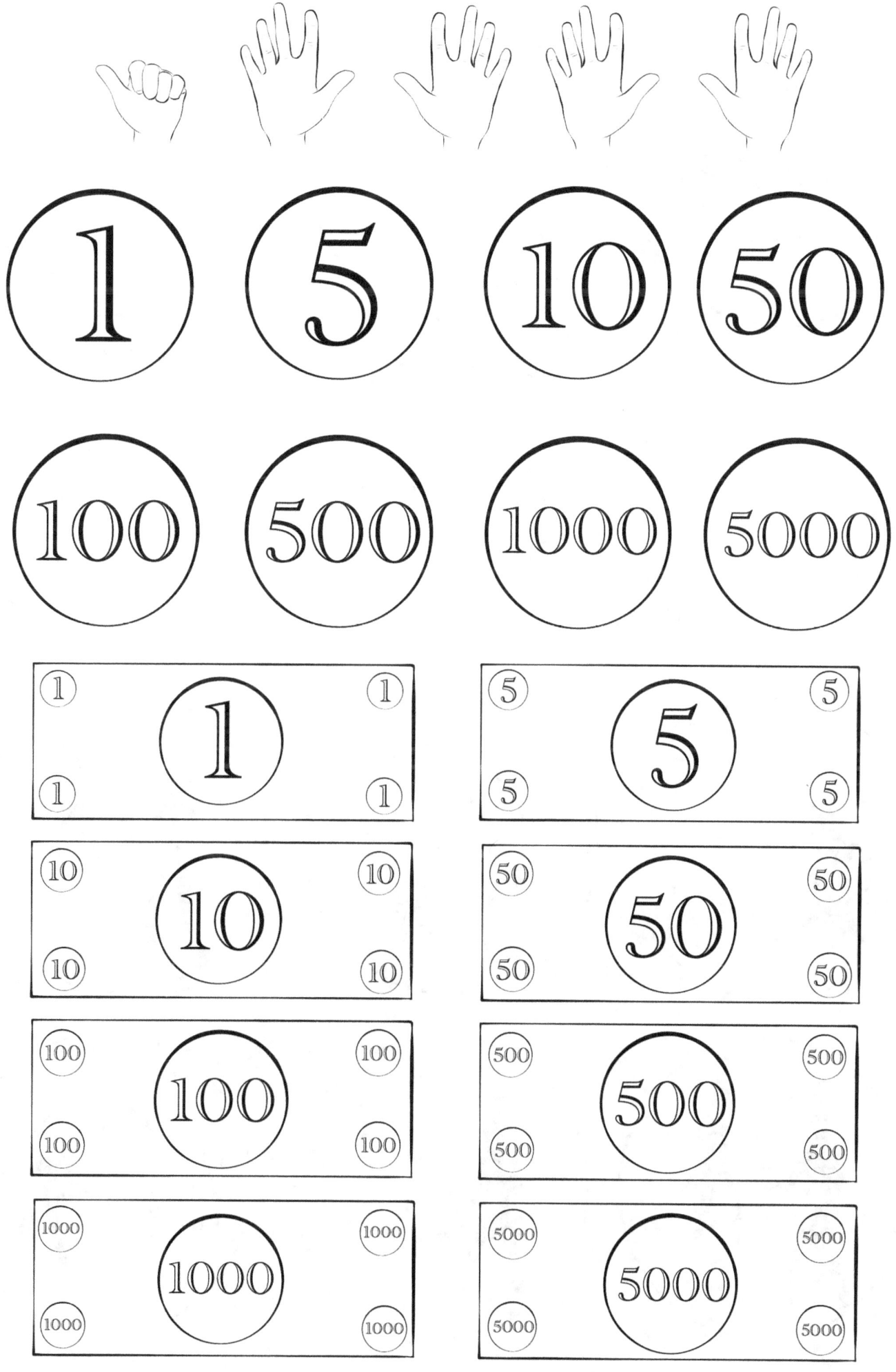

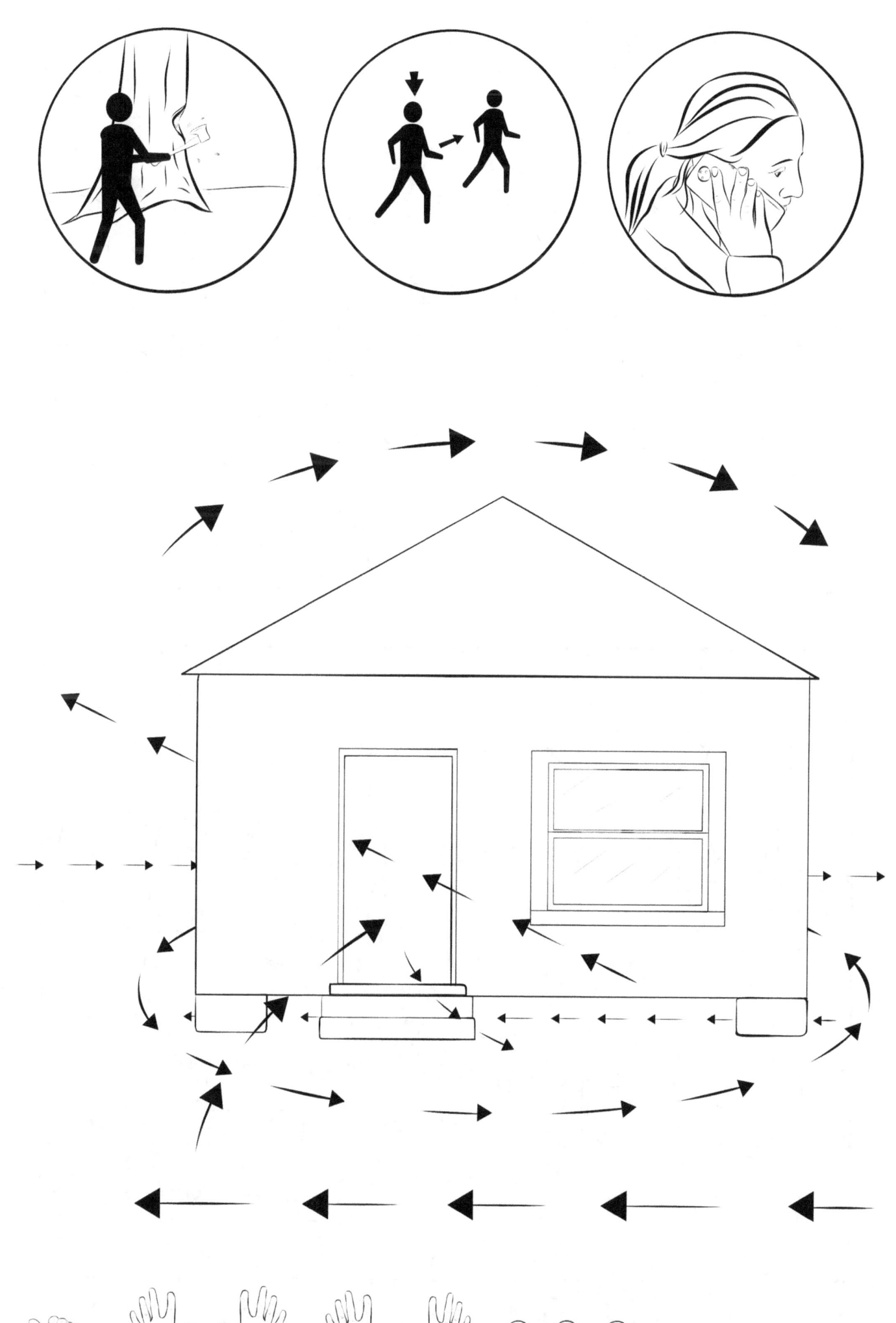

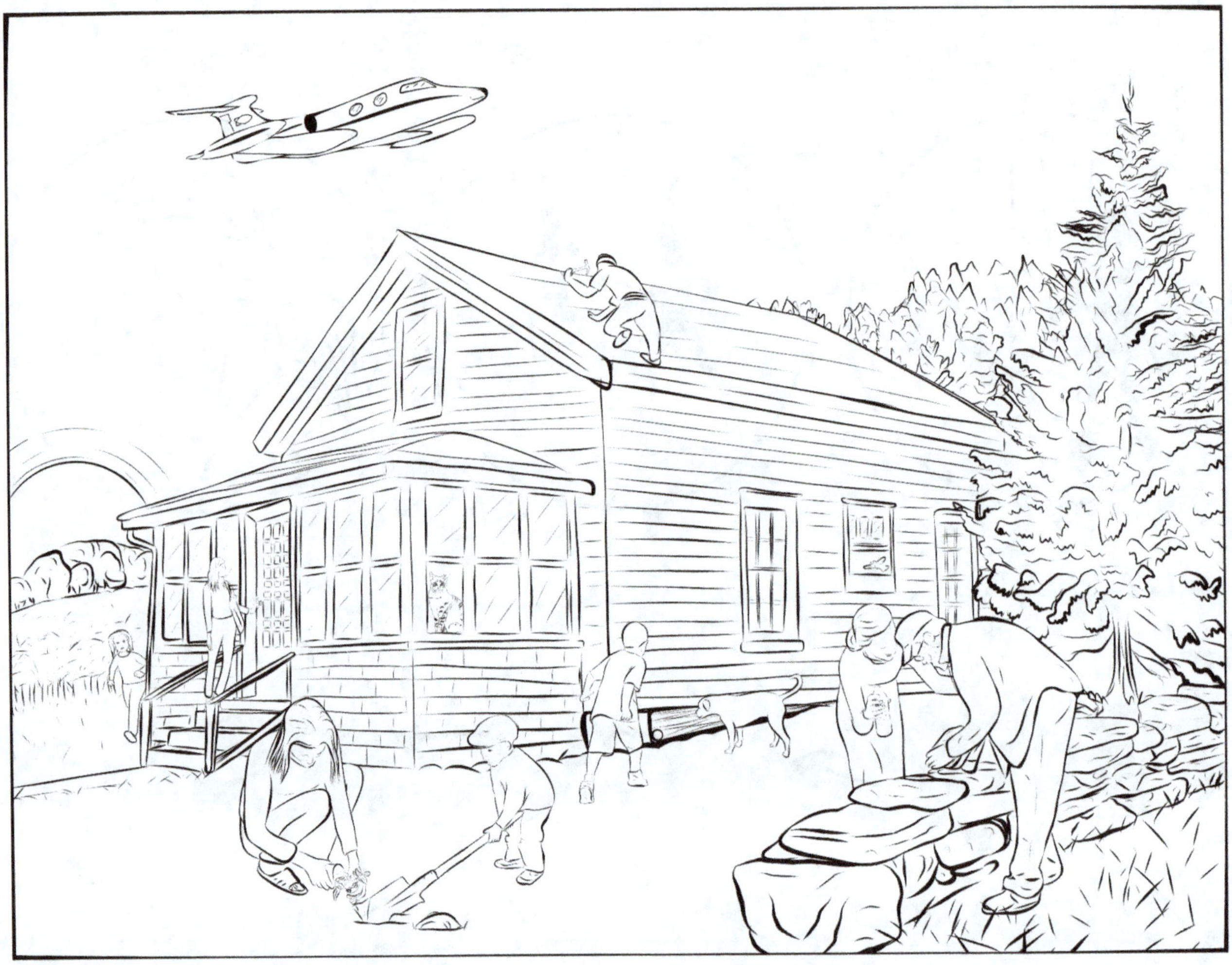

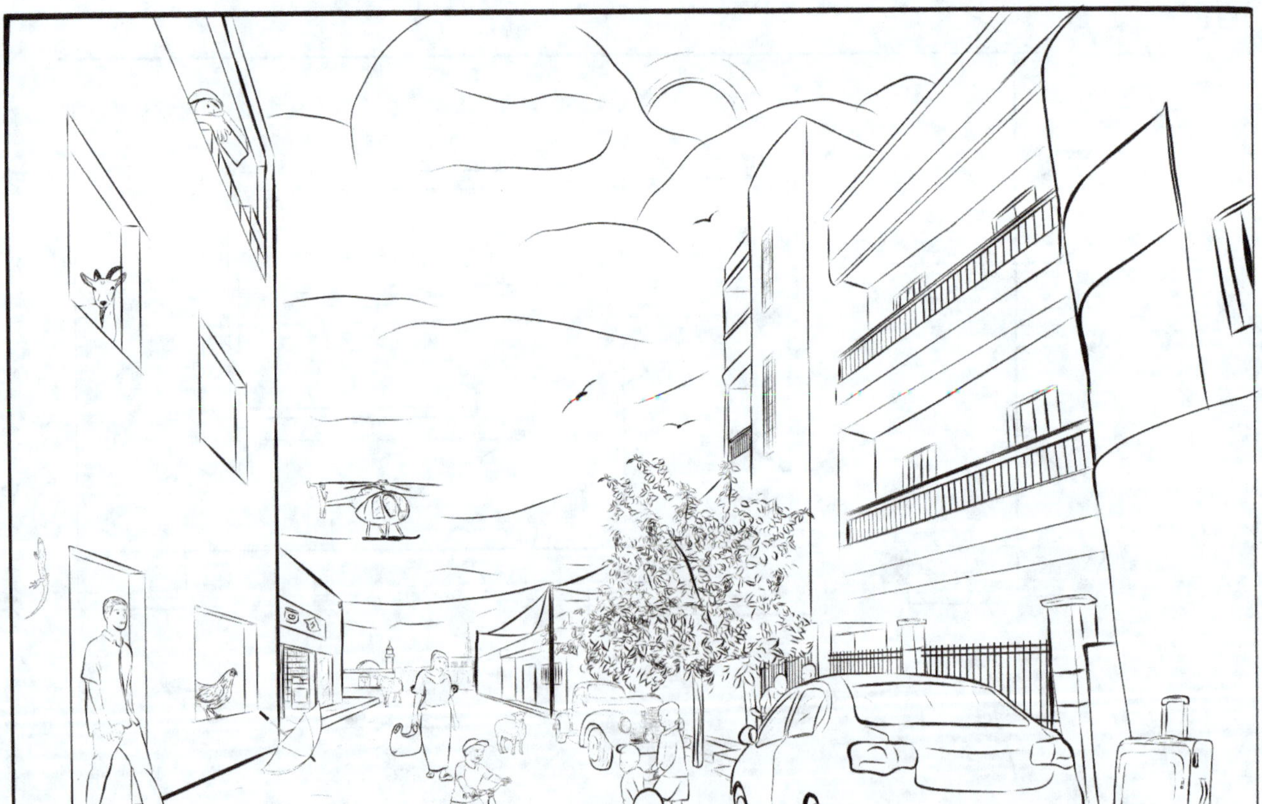

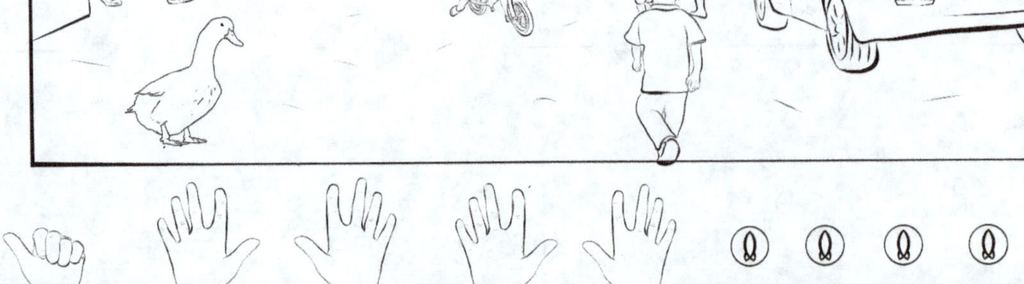

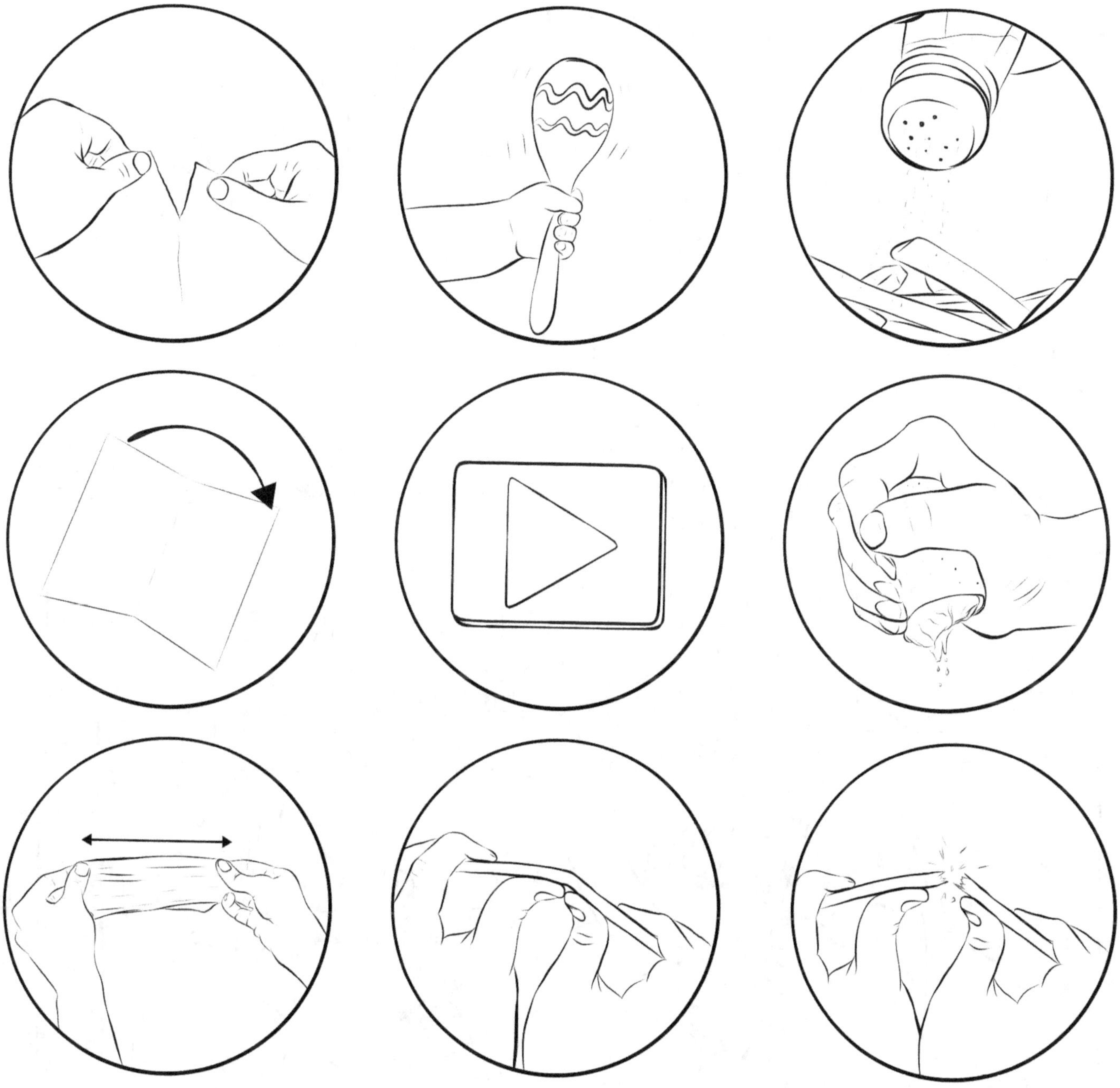

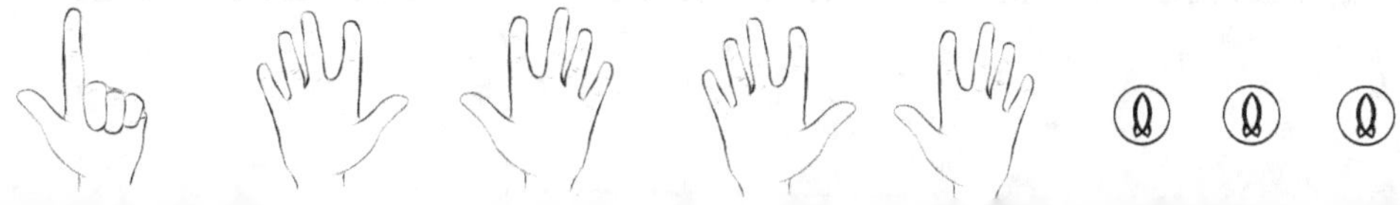

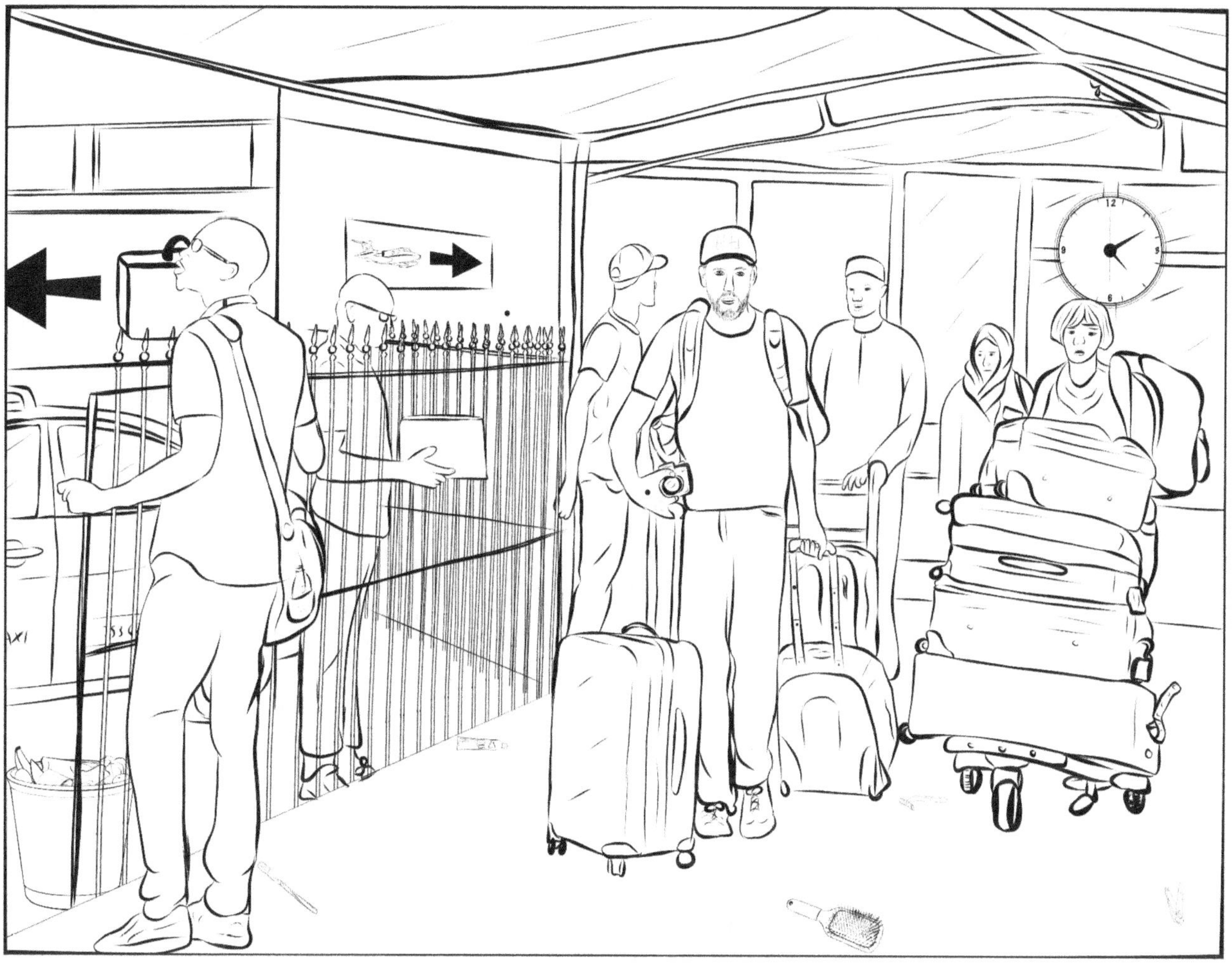

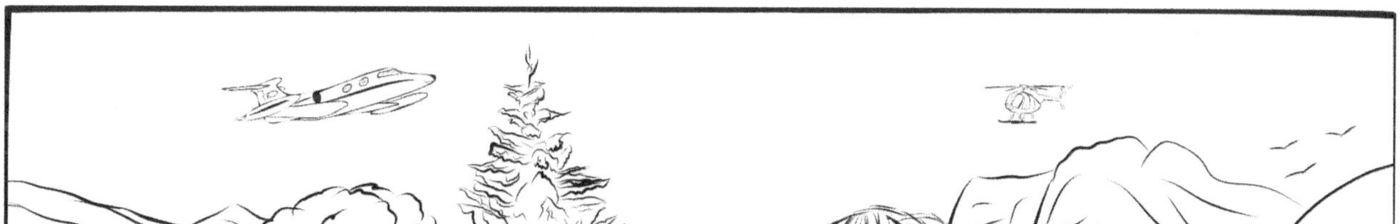

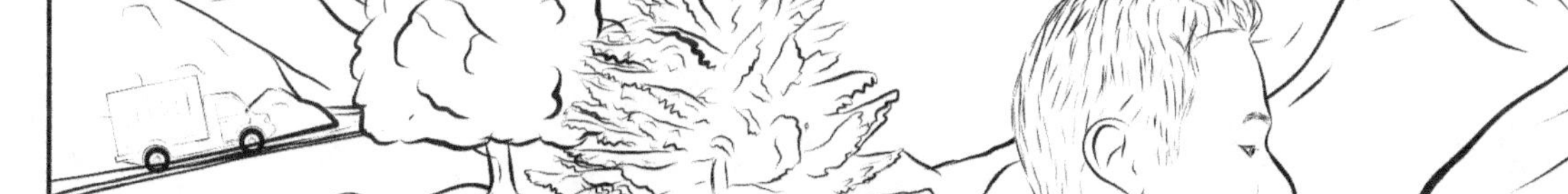

www.ingramcontent.com/pod-product-compliance
Lightning Source LLC
Chambersburg PA
CBHW080852120626
46546CB00009B/2803